Scripture Comes to Life: Reflections on Biblical Wisdom in Everyday Experience is a gem of a gift to those who desire more intimate fellowship with God. Author Ruth Stitt, a licensed counselor, ordained minister, worship leader, and passionate follower of Jesus, has written a timeless treasure of essays just as applicable to seekers as to seasoned believers in Christ. Masterfully crafted, this book brilliantly melds the Word of God with pearls of wisdom gleaned through a lifetime of putting the teachings of Jesus into practice. Not a cumbersome theological treatise but a winsomely engaging compilation of life lessons, *Scripture Comes to Life* beckons the reader to pull up a chair and join Jesus and the author in the journey of a lifetime.

—The Rev. Jan de Chambrier,
author, minister, missionary

"An intriguing tapestry of Scripture, thought, emotion, lessons learned, and taught. Ruth Stitt weaves God's word, faith, discipleship, grace, grieving, sobriety, therapy, therapist, and theologian into a beautiful vision of an applied daily walk with God. "

—Chris Holland, D.Min.,
pastor and police chaplain

SCRIPTURE
Comes to
LIFE

*Reflections on Biblical Wisdom
in Everyday Experience*

RUTH E. STITT

CONTENTS

SCRIPTURE COMES TO LIFE

Years ago, I fell in love with the words of Scripture before becoming acquainted with their author. I was raised to value education, literature, and learning. As soon as someone pointed me to the Bible in my twenties, I found it incredibly deep, rich, exciting, and compelling, and studying it thoroughly became my passionate pursuit.

Before long I was convinced that the book contained much more than literature. It was a source of life-giving, sanity-restoring truth, leading me to the ultimate source of grace and truth, Jesus Christ. My devotion to the Word of God continues to this day and will endure, I'm sure, until I cross over the great divide.

It is easy to overlook or take for granted the many ways that engagement with the Bible transforms the mind, the worldview, and even the way the brain works under its influence. The stories, characters, and teachings of the Bible become such a part of the psyche that they influence every part of life. The protagonists feel like intimate friends; we so often read of their exploits and imagine ourselves there, observing or even participating in the story.

We are listening in on Eve's conversation with a beguiling serpent, or trudging up Mt. Moriah with Abraham and Isaac, carrying kindling for the sacrifice. We are mourning with Job as he scratches himself with shards of pottery or trembling next to Esther before the scepter of the king. We are with Ruth, gleaning in the harvest fields of Boaz, or with David, writing poetry by the springs of En Gedi.

We are with Jesus, fighting sleep as he cries out to his Father under the ancient olive trees.

The history of God's people becomes our story, and we lay claim to their covenant promises. As sons and daughters of Abraham, we seek to take hold, like Paul, of "that for which Christ took hold" of us (Phil. 3:12). We marvel at the excruciating beauty of Jesus's life and the horror of a death that accomplished the redemption of the world. We receive the doctrines and admonitions delivered to the church as our manual for Christian living amid a crooked and depraved world. With the guidance of the Holy Spirit, even the fine points of Jewish law in Leviticus or the genealogies of Matthew can come alive and find relevance in our daily affairs.

I have come to realize that this makes people like me rather odd in a culture that heaps contempt on the ancient faith. We are strangers, aliens who seek "a better country, that is, a heavenly one" (Heb. 11:16 ESV). In my own experience, even family members who have known me all my life and are very dear to me cannot relate to the vast landscape of biblical experience in my imagination, the lens through which I view all else. Like those returning from exotic travel adventures, we can tell stories and show pictures, but there are some things each person must experience for himself or herself.

In the meantime, having been so impacted by my travels in the pages of the Book, I find myself with culture shock as I navigate American culture in the twenty-first century. I want desperately to share my experience of the Word of God with those who have never viewed its magnificence.

Scripture's perfect wisdom compels us to be witnesses to the reality and applicability of its truth. But we must share this awareness of another world gently and kindly, never letting it become a bludgeon, a battering ram, or a barrier. We share our stories, pictures, and experiences with our Lord and King in hopes that it will inspire and motivate others to embark on their own journey of discovery.

That has been my heart and intention as I've written my blog, called *Scripture Comes to Life*, and other published articles over the last few years. In my daily reading of Scripture, I ask the Holy Spirit to reveal something fresh—a phrase, an image, a principle, a metaphor—for me to study more deeply and then share with my readers. I try to put myself in the scenes and contexts I'm reading about so that I might literally "see" something that can be explored and applied to our contemporary lives as lovers of God.

Some of these essays are very personal, as I share from my own experiences as a woman, a wife, a mother, a sister, a friend, a musician, and a dog-lover. Each of these aspects of my personal journey has brought Scripture to life in delightful and challenging ways. As I am now in my sixties, many of these revelations have been poignant and precious to me, and I pray that you will also find them meaningful.

I have devoted some chapters to considering what devoted discipleship looks like in a corrupted world system. How are we to function in the world without becoming like the world? This question turns our focus to matters of the heart, our spiritual practices, and our ministries in the church and in the world. One chapter specifically addresses our unavoidable encounters with grief, temptation, and suffering. Discipleship includes some hard things.

Other essays reflect ideas I've learned and taught in my work as a minister, professional counselor, and educator over the years. I share principles and wisdom that intersect with Scripture in intriguing ways. I've come to value the integration of psychology, sociology, biology, and ethics with what used to be considered the "queen" of all sciences, theology. This brings a well-rounded, commonsense perspective on our life as spiritual beings having a human experience.

I have been bold at times, meddling in the distorted value systems I see being lived out in our world. But in those cases, my goal is to challenge, not to offend. Challenged people are open to growth and change; offended people are more likely to turn away and become resistant to the message. I hope that I have been successful in holding to this goal and that you are reading this because you are in the first category. Thank you for joining me on the journey where Scripture comes to life in remarkable ways!

1

IN JESUS CHRIST

I t is an immeasurable blessing that we have available to us four gospels containing the stories of the life of our Lord Jesus Christ. We know of his miraculous conception, his birth, his baptism and entry into ministry, and his travels around the Holy Land. We have eyewitness accounts of his arrest, trials, his Passion, death, and resurrection. We even have his teachings after walking out of the tomb!

We learn so much, not only from his teaching but also from his way of being. We can observe the way he responded to conflict, questions, and challenges to his authority. We see what it looks like to live in a way that is holy and pleasing to the Father in every way.

These essays are reflections on various events, miracles, conversations, and lessons from the life of Jesus. I like to imagine that his story is a sweeping screenplay, and I have a bit part. I invite you to do the same. Zoom out to survey the sweeping panorama of the life of the Messiah. Zoom in to examine the finer points of his teachings, wisdom from the greatest rabbi who ever walked the earth. To borrow from a proverb, it is as though we are following Jesus so closely that as he walks through that ancient land, the dust he stirs falls upon us.

ASKING THE RIGHT QUESTIONS

Jesus was brilliant. Even at the young age of 12, he slipped away from his family to debate with his elders in the religious establishment of the temple. He astonished them with his answers, and with his questions.

A mark of true wisdom and intelligence is the ability to ask good questions. When his parents tracked Jesus down and scolded him, he replied, "Why were you searching for me? Didn't you know that it was necessary for me to be in my Father's house?" (Luke 2:49 CSB). Jesus even responded to his parents' questions with questions!

I'm a parent, and I remember how the seemingly endless questions from my kids at certain ages wore me out but I was glad that they want so badly to understand things, so I dared not shut the questions down. I've also been a college professor and can attest to how refreshing and invigorating it is when students ask questions that contribute to the learning of all.

For Jesus, the teaching aspect of his mere three years of active ministry was marked by some of the most provocative questions ever posed. He refused to conform to religious tradition at any point where it betrayed the Word of God, so he never took the bait from the legalists. On many occasions, when he discerned an ulterior motive behind a question, he would answer with another question. This either diverted the conversation, elicited a teaching parable, or called out hypocrisy and error in the questioner.

When asked, Should we pay taxes to Caesar? Jesus asked, "Whose image is this? And whose inscription?" (Matt. 22:20). When asked, "Is it lawful to heal on the Sabbath?" Jesus asked, "If any of you has a sheep and it falls into a pit on the Sabbath, will you not take hold of it and lift it out?" (Matt. 12:11). When asked, "Who is my neighbor?" Jesus asked (after telling the story of the Good Samaritan), "Which of these three do you think was a neighbor to the man who fell into the hands of robbers?" (Luke 10:46).

When asked, "Good teacher, what good deed must I do to inherit eternal life?" Jesus asked, "Why are you asking Me about what is good?" (Matt. 19:16–17). When asked, "Why do your disciples break the tradition of the elders? They don't wash their hands before they eat!" Jesus asked, "And why do you break the command of God for the sake of your tradition?" (Matt. 15:2–3). These are only a few among so many examples.

We also observe that when someone asked a question with a sincere, seeking heart of faith, Jesus was willing to answer directly and compassionately. When the Pharisee Nicodemus came secretly at night and asked Jesus, "How can someone be born when they are old?" Jesus answered, "Very truly I tell you, no one can enter the kingdom of God unless they are born of water and the Spirit" (John 3:4–5). He expounded fully on this theme, discerning that Nicodemus genuinely wanted to know. This is the passage that surrounds our beloved John 3:16.

The woman at the well also asked valid questions, such as, "You are a Jew and I am a Samaritan woman. How can you ask me for a drink?" To which Jesus replied, "If you knew the gift of God and who it is that asks you for a drink, you would have asked him and he would have given you living water." Her follow-up questions: "Where can you get this living water? Are you greater than our father Jacob who gave us this well?" Jesus replied, "Everyone who drinks this water will be thirsty again, but whoever drinks the water I give them will never thirst. Indeed, the water I give them will become in them a spring of water welling up to eternal life" (John 4:7–13). Genuine, well-formed questions elicited genuine, well-formed answers.

In this life of faith, it is not wrong to have questions, even really big ones. In fact, we could argue that questioning is essential to an authentic and mature faith. Evangelists present the gospel to the lost, often responding to unasked questions, and bringing them to a point of repentance and the decision to follow Christ. Once the lost become "found," the apologists and disciple-makers take over, answering the very legitimate questions that arise as new converts attempt to properly interpret and apply the word of truth.

Nicodemus and the woman at the well revealed from their questions that they were ready to become disciples. They just needed a bit more understanding about the kingdom of God. Jesus was happy to engage with them. He will do the same with us.

Most of the Pharisees of Jesus's day completely missed this, and therefore missed the opportunity to take into their hearts the Messiah's wisdom from heaven. Their hearts were warped, and so they asked wrongheaded, hard-hearted questions. Jesus didn't fall into their traps.

Lord, help us to have pure, sincere hearts and minds that ask the right questions of you. And help us to present your truthful answers when people ask the right questions of us.

BLINDNESS AND SIGHT

*"For judgment I have come into this world, so that the
blind will see and those who see will become blind."*

John 9:39

The story of Jesus healing a blind man in John 9 communicates
an essential truth about true blindness and true sight. Blindness
and sight are determined not only by how well our physical eyes are
functioning. We see with our minds and our hearts.

The story involves a very mixed and conflicted cast of characters. First, there is Jesus. Walking along with his disciples, Jesus saw
a man who had been blind from birth. The disciples posed the question, "Why was this man born blind? Was it because of his own sins
or his parents' sins?"

Jesus answered that sin was not at issue in this case, but the power
that God was about to reveal. "The night is coming, and then no
one can work. But while I am here in the world, I am the light of
the world." Even if a man born blind might regain his sight—as this
man was about to do—he would not see rightly without receiving
Jesus, the light of the world.

Jesus made a mudpack with dirt and spit, rubbed it on the man's
eyes, and sent him to rinse it off in the pool of Siloam. Lo and behold,
he returned seeing! The whole community rejoiced and celebrated
wildly, right? Sadly, that's not the direction the story takes.

Many claimed to be confused about the man's identity. Could it
be someone who looked like him? No, the man insisted that he was

the same person they had seen begging in that spot for years. He told them plainly how his healing had occurred. It was because of "the man they call Jesus."

Wanting to confront Jesus, the skeptics discovered he had already moved on. The neighbors dragged the healed man to the Pharisees "because it was on the Sabbath that Jesus had made the mud and healed him." Unbelievably, this was the aspect of the event that concerned them most.

The man gave his testimony about Jesus again. The facts were plain to see. But those facts presented the religious folks with a huge problem, a spiritual conundrum, a riddle to solve. Some said, "This man Jesus is not from God, for he is working on the Sabbath." Others asked, "But how could an ordinary sinner do such miraculous signs?" They were divided in their opinions.

The Pharisees asked the formerly blind man's opinion of what had happened. He reasoned that Jesus must be a prophet to carry such power. The Pharisees bristled at this conclusion.

Enter the man's parents, the next witnesses interrogated by the Pharisees. "Is this your son? Was he born blind? If so, how can he now see?" These parents might be the saddest characters in the story. Can you imagine having a son blind from birth? All his life he is dependent, relying on the pity of others. Suddenly he can see! What a game-changer! Wouldn't you want to shout from the mountaintop and tell the whole world?

Instead, these parents feared the Jewish leaders, who "had announced that anyone saying Jesus was the Messiah would be expelled from the synagogue." Even acknowledging a sign and a miracle accomplished by Jesus was a basis for excommunication. God's power was not allowed in their midst. It interfered with their religion. The parents replied, "He is old enough to speak for himself; ask him."

The Pharisees put the man with new sight on the stand again, urging him to recant his testimony, insisting, "This man Jesus is a sinner." But the man refused to budge from giving credit to Jesus. As they say, you can argue with someone's theology, but it is hard to argue with an experience.

This man had admirable boldness and tenacity. "Look! I told you once. Didn't you listen? Why do you want to hear it again? Do you want to become his disciples too?" This was a slap in their faces! He continued,

> "I know this: I was blind, and now I can see…. Ever since the world began, no one has been able to open the eyes of someone born blind. If this man were not from God, he couldn't have done it." (v. 32 NLT)

At this point, the leaders shut down the discussion by insulting him, calling him an ignorant sinner, and throwing him out of the synagogue.

John 9 ends with another encounter between Jesus and the man who had received his sight. This time Jesus speaks with him about faith. "Do you believe in the Son of Man?…You have *seen* him and he is speaking to you." The man's heartfelt response: "'Yes, Lord, I believe!' And he worshiped Jesus" (vv. 36–38 NLT, emphasis added).

This gospel story speaks clearly about the fallibility of opinions and the problem of spiritual blindness. It reveals the tragic folly of those who dogmatically adhere only to facts that fit into their preconceived religious boxes. Spiritual pride has a way of leading people to assume they're seeing clearly when they are not.

Our God-given free will entitles us to our own opinions about Jesus Christ. But the only opinion that matters in the end is the Father's opinion of his Son, and the Father has already declared that he is "well pleased" with him. Jesus can save, heal, and deliver at any time, on any day, in any place, and in any manner he chooses. Coming into agreement with that opinion is the way we receive our sight.

Healing of the Blind Man by Jesus Christ, by Carl Block, 1570–1575

COME, LISTEN, FOLLOW

Two teachings of Jesus in the Gospel of Luke plainly reveal that our salvation in Christ must lead to corresponding actions. When it does, it results in our growth in wisdom and represents him well to the world.

The first is the well-known parable of the two types of builders in Luke 6:46–49 (NLT):

> "So why do you keep calling me 'Lord, Lord!' when you don't do what I say? I will show you what it's like when someone *comes to me, listens to my teaching, and then follows it.* It is like a person building a house who digs deep and lays the foundation on solid rock. When the floodwaters rise and break against that house, it stands firm because it is well built. But anyone who hears and doesn't obey is like a person who builds a house right on the ground, without a foundation. When the floods sweep down against that house, it will collapse into a heap of ruins." (emphasis added)

Powerful words! Notice that the first verb is *come.* There is nothing to build, and nothing to build upon, until we first come humbly to God to receive his grace in salvation. At this point, the work is on God's part because we are incapable of being saved by our own works. He draws us, and when we hear the good news and receive it into our hearts, our part is to trust that it is true. God then positions us upon the foundation of Jesus Christ. There is no other firm foundation (1 Cor. 3:11).

The second action is to *listen*. After salvation, we enter the training academy of Jesus. He becomes our rabbi and teacher, and we come under the yoke of his teaching. We take it in daily by reading it, hearing it, speaking it, singing it, meditating on it, memorizing it, praying through it. It truly becomes the air we breathe or our daily bread, as the song says.

But…if we stop at the point of listening, we do not progress toward wisdom and godliness. Jesus rebuked those who hear his word but don't obey it. Whatever they think they are building will not stand when a storm comes. I like the paraphrase of Luke 6:46–49 in The Message:

> "These words I speak to you are not mere additions to your
> life, homeowner improvements to your standard of living. They are foundation words, words to build a life on."

When we receive his teachings, we don't treat them as a magic formula for self-improvement. His words, revealed by the Spirit and Word of God, are the basis of all our decisions and choices, our work, our play, our spending, our investments in life. There is no part of life in which his truth is not considered. The Passion Translation adds this emphasis to the passage:

> "If you just use my words in Bible studies and don't work
> them into your life, you are like a dumb carpenter who
> built a house but skipped the foundation."

This is why Jesus says there is no point in calling him Lord if we don't do what he says!

The second passage is embedded in Luke 7. Jesus responds to messengers sent by John the Baptist seeking assurances that he was the Messiah. He gives them a message for John, pointing to his ministry of healing and preaching:

> "The blind receive their sight, the lame walk, those with leprosy are cleansed, the deaf hear, the dead are raised, and the poor are told the good news." (Luke 7:22–23 CSB)

Jesus claimed that his deeds spoke for themselves. This clues us in on the works he expects us to pursue after we have made him Lord.

Jesus knew that some people would be convinced that he was Messiah and others would be offended, so he added, "Blessed is the one who isn't offended by me" (Lk.7:23, CSB). If we can't get past being offended, we may miss the blessings of being permanently attached to the kingdom of Christ.

What follows is a bit puzzling in the King James Version, which reads, "Wisdom is vindicated by all her children." Other translations add nuances, such as "The proof of wisdom is in the kinds of people it produces" (CJB); "Wisdom is shown to be right by what its followers do" (CEV); "Wisdom is shown to be right by the lives of those who follow it" (NLT); "The wisdom of God will be proven true by the expressions of godliness in everyone who follows me" (TPT); and "A man is proved wise by what he has done"(WEB).

In all these interpretations, it is in doing right and showing godly character that we display what we are building, and upon what we are building. The Message mixes in more metaphor: "Opinion polls don't count for much, do they? The proof of the pudding is in the eating."

These teachings are confirmed in the epistles. Paul states that after receiving revelation that we are Christ's image-bearers, we move from "glory to glory" as we reflect him in the world (2 Cor. 3:18). We are to consistently remember and represent his goodness, compassion, wisdom, and zeal for God. We put truth into motion by doing good.

Peter asserts repeatedly that our works of righteousness will get the attention of the world, even arousing persecution by people who are offended by Christ and his message (1 Peter 3). James argues, "Faith without works is dead" (James 2:20 KJV). We understand that he is not promoting works-based salvation but observing that our works are how our faith becomes developed and evident to others. We become people who look just like Jesus because we do as he does. We become people with sturdy, beautiful lives built upon an indestructible foundation, and nothing in this world can tear us down.

We come to Jesus with humble hearts, listen intently to his words, and diligently, daily put them into practice. Then we are shown to be wise and can truly call him Lord.

WHAT MADE JESUS
MAD—AND STILL DOES

Jesus was a remarkably patient man—perfectly patient, you might say. He was especially patient and kind toward those who were slow to understand or had any form of incapacity. He explained things repeatedly, he told stories, and he gave illustrations, as we do with children to teach and discipline them. This demonstrated his lovely patience.

But there were times when Jesus got truly angry. People often point to the account in John 2 when looking for a picture of an angry Jesus. Jesus stormed through the temple courts with a whip, turning over tables and making a scene. People sometimes like to compare their own righteous indignation to his. If Jesus got that angry, people say, it is OK to subject people to their rage.

We need to take care with our interpretation and application. This is the only time recorded in Scripture when Jesus behaved in this way. Because we know that he only did what he saw the Father doing, there must have been a specific, God-ordained reason for that dramatic display of his outrage. This is a topic that deserves a whole chapter.

But while discussing what made Jesus mad—and still does—we don't take this occasion out of the larger context of his ministry. There were other occasions when Jesus expressed anger differently, in response to words, works, and attitudes that displeased him. I argue that if these things made him mad during his earthly ministry, they are still displeasing to him as a risen Savior.

Human anger is usually a response to a threat, and we sometimes need this emotion for our survival. When someone threatens our safety, our loved ones, our property, or our sense of fairness, anger is the usual God-given response. Sometimes anger motivates us to take action to rescue or protect others who are facing such threats.

Child pornography should make us truly angry. Trafficking human beings should make us furious. Racial prejudice and discrimination should move us to seek justice. Rampant contempt for the lives of preborn babies should keep us awake at night with outrage. These are egregious offenses against any value system that prioritizes mercy and justice.

Throughout the Gospels, Jesus reveals his value system and priorities, as well as how and when it is appropriate to be angry. He didn't get angry for anger's sake. And we, as lovers of God, don't act out in anger to satisfy our carnal craving for vengeance. To the contrary. We should be moved with anger when we experience threats to the true and loving values of his kingdom, in which faith, justice, and mercy prevail. When there are serious attacks on these kingdom values, we are to channel our anger in ways that are pleasing to him. To guide us, these are five categories of behavior or attitude that made Jesus angry, and how he responded:

Faithlessness. Sometimes Jesus's disciples reacted with fear and unbelief to situations in which he wanted to see courage and faith. On a number of occasions, Jesus got frustrated when they could or would not exercise the authority he had imparted to them. One example is when they couldn't cast a demon out of a child. He rebuked them, saying, "You unbelieving and perverse generation…how long shall I stay with you? How long shall I put up with you? Bring the boy here to me" (Matt. 17:17). Can't you imagine him sighing deeply? It bothers Jesus when we don't walk in the fullness of our faith.

Exploitation of the poor and weak. This one covers a lot of situations in the Gospels and in our world. Jesus warned his audiences against doing anything to destroy the innocent. In Capernaum, he declared that they'd be better off tying a huge millstone around their necks and jumping into the lake than to have to face the coming judgment for those who bring harm to children or other defenseless people. Jesus despised arrogance, self-righteousness, or power-grabbing at the expense of the humble and vulnerable.

Empty religion and hypocrisy. Matthew 23 includes an extensive discourse on this topic. He called the religious legalists of his day vipers, hypocrites, and blind guides, men who talked a good game but whose actions belied their professions of righteousness. He compared them to "whitewashed sepulchers…full of dead men's bones" (v. 27 KJV). He despised their practice of keeping appearances of religious scrupulosity when he knew their hearts were wicked, proud, greedy, and perverse.

Love of money/materialism. A central tenet of Jesus's gospel is letting go of our attachments to worldly wealth and our preoccupation with money. The cost for being his disciple was (and is) a willingness to surrender all to him. Jesus seems to have been righteously indignant toward people who claimed to be devoted to him but were unwilling to sacrifice their wealth and comfort in order to devote themselves to his kingdom and his righteousness.

Misusing Scripture to prop up or justify any or all the above. Jesus indicted the religious leaders and teachers of the Law for missing the essential truths and prophesies of God's Word. On one occasion, when the Pharisees attempted to trip up Jesus in his doctrine, he answered them, "Ye do err, not knowing the scriptures, nor the power of God" (Matt. 22:29 KJV). To paraphrase Jesus: "Don't quote the Word to me if you have no fear of God and only want to prove yourself right."

Most of these behaviors and attitudes were present when Jesus tore through the temple that day. At risk was the faith of the common people, their financial exploitation by the religious establishment, and the bringing of sacrifices without a corresponding sincerity of faith, corrupting God's holy place with commercialism.

Jesus is still alive, and I assume these things still displease and anger him when they occur in our lives, whether we are the perpetrators or the victims. He loves us without conditions. If we want to know what does please our Lord, we simply need to flip these attitudes and behaviors around and seek the opposite. This is what we will do next.

WHAT MADE JESUS GLAD—AND STILL DOES

We've examined some words, works, and attitudes that made Jesus mad, and now we will observe from the Gospels what made him glad. As in the previous study, I argue that if certain behaviors or attitudes were pleasing to Jesus while he was here as a man, they please him today as resurrected Savior. What puts a smile on his face and joy in his heart?

Faith. As much as Jesus could get aggravated with people when they succumbed to fear, he delighted when they showed bold faith. The centurion who believed in Jesus's power to heal his servant from a distance by simply saying a word is a wonderful example (Matt. 8:5–10). Jesus told Thomas the doubter, "Because you have seen me, you have believed; blessed are those who have not seen and yet have believed" (John 20:29). Jesus seems to get really jazzed when we walk by faith in the miraculous and don't rely only on our physical senses to define reality.

Generosity. Jesus commended an elderly widow who put her small coins in the offering. He knew that in her sacrificial giving she did not seek the praise of men, but the rewards of heaven (Mark 12:41–44). He argued with a rich young ruler that he would find salvation and satisfaction by giving away his possessions to the poor (Luke 18:22). Jesus was happy when people were willing to give anything and everything away to become true followers of his way of life. He taught that the best thing to do with worldly wealth is to give it to those who are in need. This brings freedom from attachment to the world, and freedom brings joy.

True Worship. Hear these words to Simon, the self-righteous Pharisee who had invited Jesus to dinner in his home, as a sinful woman poured out her worship at Jesus's feet:

> "Do you see this woman? I came into your house. You did not give me any water for my feet, but she wet my feet with her tears and wiped them with her hair. You did not give me a kiss, but this woman, from the time I entered, has not stopped kissing my feet. You did not put oil on my head, but she has poured perfume on my feet. Therefore, I tell you, her many sins have been forgiven—as her great love has shown. But whoever has been forgiven little loves little" (Luke 7:44–46).

Jesus said that this woman's deed would be spoken of wherever the gospel was preached, until the end of time. He was moved and impressed by her unbridled devotion. He said that the Father is looking for such worshippers, those who worship in Spirit and in truth (John 4:24).

Childlike innocence. Jesus did not select wise, learned people to be his closest disciples. He chose fishermen, tax collectors, ordinary working-class men and women. How he rejoiced in the Father's plan to reveal the greatest mysteries to those with the faith of children (Matt. 11:25–26)! Why did Jesus say that we have to become like children to enter the kingdom? Because little children are innocent and simple, with hearts not yet hardened by the sin or wickedness of the world. Jesus beckoned the children to come sit in his lap so he could bless them. He found joy in their company. Likewise, he rejoices when we come to him with this simplicity of heart.

Obedience to his teaching. Jesus was deeply knowledgeable of the Scriptures from his youth and quoted Scripture constantly—the Torah, the prophets, and the writings. He knew them inside and out and insisted on their proper, Spirit-led interpretation. Jesus rejoiced when people responded in obedience to his revelations of truth. A pastor friend of mine likes to say, "Obedience is God's love language." Jesus says, "Learn from me, for I am gentle and humble in heart, and you will find rest for your souls" (Matt. 11:29).

Being true to ourselves. You may remember the scene in *Chariots of Fire* when Eric Liddell acknowledged that God had called him as a missionary, but observed that God had also given him the ability to run fast, and said, "When I run, I feel his pleasure." Each disciple of Jesus has a distinct identity and calling in Christ. At the heart of our mission on this earth is to find the thing he has created and equipped us to do and get busy doing it.

Jesus told Peter not to be preoccupied with someone else's assignment or destiny. He said simply, "You must follow me" (John 21:22). Follow me, Peter—with all your strengths, and in all of your weaknesses—keep being you, and by all means, keep following me.

Jesus still beckons us to believe without having to see, to give generously, to worship unreservedly, to come near like children, to walk in the light of his teaching, and to bring our best, most authentic selves as we follow and serve. He loves us without conditions, but Scripture shows us that doing these things makes him glad!

THREE DISCIPLESHIP
LESSONS FROM
THE RISEN LORD

There are three lessons in the gospel of John that stand out as especially significant instruction. Because they were spoken after Jesus's resurrection, they are words imbued with profound meaning and authority, spoken from the other side of the tomb.

First, there is a lesson about faith. Jesus admonishes Thomas for refusing to believe in his resurrection until he sees it for himself. He commends those who believe without having to see: "Because you have seen me, you have believed; blessed are those who have not seen and yet have believed" (John 20:29). If we are to walk in a manner pleasing to the Lord, as true disciples, we do not wait for physical evidence of his grace, his power, his purpose. We seek truth moment by moment, responding in obedience to the Holy Spirit's leadership. We do this whether we understand it or not, and whether we see physical evidence of his presence or not.

The second is a lesson about not dwelling in the past or worrying about the future. Jesus says to Peter, "When you were young, you were able to do as you liked; you dressed yourself and went wherever you wanted to go. But when you are old, you will stretch out your hands, and others will dress you and take you where you don't want to go" (John 21:18 NLT). Applying this to ourselves, we are accountable not for who we were in relationship to Christ in years past, but who we are in relationship with him now.

As believers devoted to the cause of Christ, we don't simply make our own choices and go wherever we please. We make choices that are pleasing to him and only go where he calls us to go. We live in the present and look to the future. This is the only way we stay on the right path and effectively disciple others. And we do this even if it leads us on a path of suffering and death, as it did Peter.

Third is a lesson about comparison. When Peter asks Jesus about his plans for John, Jesus replies, "If I want him to remain alive until I return, what is that to you? As for you, follow me" (John 21:22 NLT). It's not our business what Jesus has planned for others, except to the extent that we can bless and encourage them to pursue those plans to the utmost. Jesus doesn't want us to compare ourselves with others or take offense if they have different callings or manners of life. It is sufficient to take heed unto ourselves (see Luke 8:18, 17:3; 1 Cor. 10:12; 1 Tim. 4:12, 16). God watches over his servants, helping us to stand secure in the place and purpose to which he has called us.

After he rose from the dead, Jesus taught his disciples that we are not to wait for physical signs to choose faith and obedience. We don't look to the past as our standard for discipleship in the present or future. And we don't seek validation by comparing our progress or purpose with others. Jesus wanted his disciples to understand these things. They are weighty, spoken by the one who conquered death.

WARMED, FRIGHTENED, OVERWHELMED BY JOY

In the last chapter of Luke's gospel (the one that merges us into chapter 1 of the book of Acts), Luke takes us from the empty tomb to a road stretching toward Emmaus, and then to Jerusalem, where Jesus reveals to his disciples that he has indeed been raised from the dead!

This is no dry recitation of history; the human emotions in the story are palpable. I looked for feeling words, and there are plenty. I am quite sure this was purposeful in the Spirit's inspiration through Luke. After the reality of Christ's crucifixion came a time of extreme anguish and terror followed by unspeakable joy and amazement.

First, there were the women who devotedly arrived at Joseph's tomb. Jesus had been laid there hastily, wrapped in linen cloths, but not yet anointed or prepared for burial. We know, of course, that by the time the women arrived he was not there. As they stood gaping at the stone that had been miraculously rolled away from the tomb's opening,

> two men suddenly appeared to them, clothed in dazzling robes. The women were *terrified* and bowed with their faces to the ground. Then the men asked, "Why are you looking in a tomb for someone who is alive? He isn't here! He is risen from the dead!" (Luke 24:4–6, NLT, emphasis added).

These wonderful lovers of Jesus of course ran back to the disciples waiting in Jerusalem to tell them what they had seen and heard. Peter and John were perplexed but ran to see for themselves.

Next there is a scene shift to the road from Jerusalem to Emmaus, where a couple of disciples encounter the risen Lord but don't recognize him. They were greatly troubled on their walk, their hopes of the Messiah's deliverance of Israel seemingly dashed after witnessing his brutal murder.

Jesus, incognito, asks them, "What are you discussing so intently as you walk along?" They stop short, *sadness* written across their faces" (24:17, NLT emphasis added). One of them, named Cleopas, tries to bring this "stranger" up to speed on current events. Instead, Jesus corrects their faulty perception of reality by presenting the entire story of redemption, starting with Moses, "explaining what all said about himself" (v. 27, NLT).

Naturally, when they get near their destination, these disciples want more of this well-informed Bible teacher's company, still not knowing his identity. Only when they get home and convince Jesus to join them for dinner do they discover who he is.

> Suddenly their eyes were opened, and they recognized him. And at that moment he disappeared! They said to each other, "Didn't our hearts *feel strangely warm* as he talked with us on the road and explained the Scriptures to us?" And within the hour they were on their way back to Jerusalem. (vv. 31–33, NLT emphasis added)

The two disciples turn right around and head back to Jerusalem. Like the women at the tomb, they have to find the guys who knew Jesus best and let them know they'd seen him.

> When they arrived, they were greeted with the report, "The Lord has really risen! He appeared to Peter." (v. 34, NLT)

Jesus had beat them to it. He'd been able to appear to all of them in different places, not bound by the constraints of time and space.

Their mutual excitement is wonderful. I wish I'd been there at that meeting! To top everything off, as they are sharing their stories, Jesus himself was suddenly standing there among them. "Peace be with you," he said. But the whole group was *terribly frightened*, thinking they were seeing a ghost! "Why are you *frightened?*" he asked. "Why do you *doubt* who I am?" (vv. 36–38, NLT, emphasis added).

Jesus shows them his hands and feet, with nail holes in them. They stand staring in disbelief, but reality hits, and they are "filled with *joy and wonder*" (v. 41, emphasis added). If we had been there, what would we want to do next? Ask him questions? Give him a big hug? Fall on our faces in worship?

> Jesus asked, "Do you have anything here to eat?" They
> gave him a piece of broiled fish (v:42).

After praying and sweating blood, being flogged and tormented, trudging to Calvary and hanging suspended in excruciating pain, dying, and rising, it turns out Jesus was a tad hungry.

But that may not have been the only reason he asked them for something to eat. Perhaps he wanted to give his followers who weren't there in person the assurance that immortal humans can still eat. That means that when our bodies take on immortality, we can eat too! I'm happy about that. I like eating—broiled fish and a thousand other things. After they had eaten and spent some more time together, he blessed them and ascended out of their sight.

> So, they worshipped him and then returned to Jerusalem
> filled with *great joy*. And they spent all of their time in the
> Temple, praising God. (vv. 52–53, NLT, emphasis added)

2

IN HIS DISCIPLES

His divine power has given us everything we need
for a godly life through our knowledge of him
who called us by his own glory and goodness.

2 Peter 1:3

Even in post-postmodern America, nearly half of those polled still say they are Christian.[1] For me, this begs the question: "What does it mean to call oneself a Christian?" Does it have the same meaning it had two thousand years ago in Antioch, when the "followers of the Way" began to be called Christians? I think not. Those Christians were disciples, known as true-blue followers of Jesus Christ, or "little Christs."

Today, the name *Christian* means many things to many people other than "little Christ." So then, whether in the first century or the twenty-first, what distinguishes a nominal Christian from a true, devoted disciple of Christ?

In my experience, some people say they are Christian because they were raised in the church, or they attend a church. Some have been baptized and may have had some religious training. Some people believe they are Christians because their family claims to be Christian, or because they live in a predominantly Christian community. These are not in themselves claims to discipleship.

The word *disciple* is obviously connected to the concept of discipline. Disciples are those who adhere to a particular teaching and way

---

1. See Amber Pariona, "Religious Demographics of the USA," World Atlas, June 26, 2018, https://www.worldatlas.com/articles/religious-composition-of-the-united-states.html.

of life. Their lifestyle, behavior, and influence reflect the teaching of the one in whom they have placed their faith and trust.

On a more serious level, disciples are those who have made Christ and their walk with him their very first priority. He is the one they live and would die for. Disciples love and serve God with all their hearts, souls, minds, and strength. And it shows.

These essays explore attributes of disciples. Scripture comes to life in many word pictures that describe the way we represent and imitate Christ in this world. We carry the Spirit and the value system of the kingdom of God, and these are ways that this distinction can be seen in us.

PURPOSEFUL

These days of angst, anger, and existential dread are trying to the soul of anyone who loves God, cares about people, pursues justice, and seeks peace. They are days of an increased sense of futility. As in the garden, our work has been cursed and plagued, and our relationships strained.

We shouldn't be surprised by this, because that is the nature of life in a fallen world. Those who are without God and without hope sometimes give up on the whole enterprise. They are consumed and destroyed by addictions and despair, even suicide.

But I've observed that even within the body of Christ, some people fare much better than others in trying times. These people usually have a clear and unshakable sense of their purpose in God while here on earth. They may flounder at times, not understanding exactly how to execute that purpose, but they never forget that God has called them to relentlessly pursue it.

When I speak of purpose in this context, I'm not referring to occupation or ministry or raising a family, as important as these things are toward *feeling* purposeful on a daily basis. I'm talking about *purpose in God*. How well are our earthly purposes aligned with the overarching purpose of God as presented in Scripture and confirmed by the Holy Spirit? How well are we as individuals, families, churches, and cultural groups fulfilling *his* purposes?

David cried out to God asking him to fulfill *his* purposes in David's life (Ps. 57:2). Solomon acknowledged the reality that we can make all kinds of plans, "but the Lord's purpose will prevail" (Prov. 19:21 NLT). When we work apart from his revealed will and desire we are apt to lament, like Isaiah: "My work seems so useless! I have spent my strength for nothing and to no purpose" (Isa. 49:4 NLT).

What, then, are God's purposes for you and me? There are many ways to answer that question, but I'll start with the purpose of Jesus Christ because he is our head and the one who calls us. He is our leader and teacher in all things. He is the author and finisher, the beginning and the end. If we mindfully and faithfully join with his purposes, we will be worthy of the name Christian: "little Christ."

Long before Christ came, Isaiah declared that the word of the Lord always hits its mark; it always accomplishes what he desires and achieves the purposes for which it was sent (Isa. 55:11). Then Jesus came, destined to fulfill every prophecy of Scripture, so that "not even the smallest detail of God's law will disappear until its purpose is achieved" (Matt. 5:18 NLT).

This is a very important clue. If we are to live within God's purpose, we must be intimately familiar with his Word, as Jesus was. This is where we find strength, hope, and courage to keep running our respective races. This is where we understand our connection to God's gigantic story of the ages, surrounded by a "cloud of witnesses" who have gone before us (Heb. 12:1).

A second clue to our purpose is found in the way Jesus draws the contrast between his purpose as our Good Shepherd and the purpose of the thief—the enemy of our souls. The thief steals, kills, and destroys what is righteous and good. Jesus's stated purpose toward his sheep "is to give them a rich and satisfying life" (John 10:10 NLT).

To receive what Jesus wants for us, we must purposefully watch with a warring vigilance that thwarts the purposes of the enemy. We must employ the spiritual weapons of praise, worship, prayer, and the spoken Word of God. Our battle is to keep our grip on the kind of life Jesus desires, a life that glorifies him in its fruitfulness and joy, even while we are at war. Oswald Chambers wrote, "God's purpose is not simply to make us beautiful, plump grapes, but to make us grapes so that He may squeeze the sweetness out of us."[1] We must be prepared to be squeezed sometimes.

Third, God has purposed for his people to represent his goodness to the world. There are many ways we can do this. But in order to come into the fullness of this purpose, we must nestle securely in the truth that God causes all things to work together for our good because we love him and have been called to his purpose (Rom. 8:28). *All things*…the good, the bad, the mad, the sad, the comedy, the tragedy, all the drama of the human experience. We trust him when we understand the whys and, more so, when we don't understand them.

Paul's writings to the church are especially helpful in understanding how we are to represent him. The message is clear. We are to fulfill our mission in Christ being "in harmony with each other…united in thought and purpose" (1 Cor. 1:10, NLT). We are to work together, each contributing to the planting and watering of the Word, encouraging each other, and reaching out to the lost (1 Cor. 3:8).

God wants us to be a suitable display of "his wisdom in its rich variety" for an audience that includes not only humans but "all the unseen rulers and authorities in the heavenly places" (Eph. 3:10, NLT). We are living displays of his goodness and wisdom! This is God's plan, and we have the privilege of walking in the center of it if we are willing. In all that we do, we seek to please God, not people (1 Thess. 2:3–5), and we hope to inspire others to seek his pleasure also.

So, whatever our individual purposes day by day, we fulfill them by staying mindful of God's greater purposes of loving and obeying his Word. We accept for ourselves and offer to others the ministry of the Good Shepherd while fighting the good fight of faith. We give unselfishly and in unity with others to build up the body of Christ and minister to those still outside of it. We get revenge on the devil by living the abundant life Christ offers and spreading it as what C. S. Lewis called a "good infection"[2] to everyone we encounter.

---

1. Oswald Chambers, My Utmost for His Highest. Ulrichsville, OH: Barbour and Company, 1963.

2. C.S. Lewis, *The Problem of Pain.* HarperCollins, 2014.

DEVOTED

We live in a time and culture of distraction. This is so much the case that there are now signs on the highways reminding drivers to avoid driving while distracted. This usually refers to texting on cell phones, but it could be eating a burrito, changing your clothes, applying mascara, disciplining your kids in the back seat, completing your tax return, etc.

It seems that some people *want* to be distracted, whether consciously or not. They might *say* that their lives are too stressful and rushed and that they would like to be able to relax and focus on only one thing at a time. But if they were to be completely honest about it, they might admit to being scared to death of what thoughts would occupy their minds if they allowed themselves to be still and listen.

Life as a disciple of Jesus should be different. It requires a measure of devotion that surpasses that which we give to any other pursuit. The distracted, busy mind is the enemy of this kind of devotional life.

In the famous account of Jesus's visit to the home of Mary and Martha, we witness Martha busily preparing a meal. She loved Jesus and wanted to be a good hostess. What was wrong with that? I would want to cook a meal for Jesus, too, and watch him enjoy it. Wouldn't you? This was Martha's ministry.

The problem was that Martha became "distracted with much serving" (Luke 10:41 KJV). This led to resentment toward her sister, who sat at the feet of Jesus, listening to his every word. Jesus commended Mary for her choice because it was a choice of devotion, not distraction. There was nothing happening for Mary that evening but being in love with her Lord. It eclipsed every other concern.

The apostle Paul illustrates the relevance of both devotion and distraction in his exposition about singleness and marriage in the kingdom of God. The married person, he asserts, is perfectly entitled to be married; a loving marriage is a blessing from God. But married people cannot devote the same attention to the ministry of the Word as their single counterparts. Married people must be concerned about worldly things, and serving the needs of their spouses, with the result that their "interests are divided" (1 Cor. 7:34). In contrast, the unmarried are free to concentrate on the Lord's business, pleasing and devoting themselves to Him fully. Paul brings no condemnation, but clarifies that whether married or single, the aim as a Christ-follower is to "live in a right way in undivided devotion to the Lord" (v.35).

"Undivided devotion to the Lord." That seems like a pretty tall order these days, doesn't it? But the Holy Spirit doesn't ask us to do things that are impossible to do. God's grace allows us to press into his rest and give him our full attention, even with other demands pressing upon us. We can be undivided, undistracted, devoted. Like Mary, we can choose the "one thing," our fascinating and worthy Lord and Savior.

Christ at the Home of Martha and Mary, Jan Vermeer, 1655

WHOLEHEARTED

Recently one of our guilty pleasures at my house has been watching *America's Got Talent.* The production design of the show is criminally noisy and garish, a great example of sensory overload for the viewer.

But we enjoy watching people who have invested tremendous time and effort pursuing their talents. Any one of them could be a poster child for wholehearted pursuit of big goals. Their stories are inspiring.

Whether it is dance, song, sport, magic, or danger, each person wants to be recognized for having achieved a level of excellence by working very hard at their given talent. I really enjoy watching people aim for their best and get rewarded for it.

Wholeheartedness goes beyond physical effort. It occupies the entire soul. It drives us beyond normalcy, mediocrity, or acceptance of limitations. Wholehearted people aren't apt to make excuses. They take responsibility for their own path, whether it leads to success or failure.

Wholeheartedness goes way beyond the performing arts. Wholehearted people are found in business, education, ministry, and even politics (sometimes). They are in every part of the world.

Please don't misunderstand me, especially you Brené Brown fans—I'm a fan too. I'm not talking about perfectionism, or obsession, or a lack of self-worth that drives people to seek significance based only on their performance in life.

I agree with Brené when she defines wholeheartedness as cultivating courage, compassion, connection, and, in our vulnerability and imperfection, "daring greatly."

Wholeheartedness, or having a whole heart, is also recognized in Scripture as a way of being and living that is commendable and honorable. It most often refers to a courageous commitment to following the righteous paths marked out by God, whatever the risks or costs.

The first people in God's story described as wholehearted were Caleb and Joshua, two of the ten spies sent by Moses on a reconnaissance mission into the Promised Land. It was called the Promised Land because the land was promised to Abraham's descendants as part of God's covenant with him. Joshua and Caleb were the only spies whose hearts were allied with the God who made that promise. All of the rest trembled in fear and cowardice.

Joshua and Caleb were the only members of their generation who lived to experience the first steps into that land forty years later. Both were granted this moment of victory because they had "followed the Lord wholeheartedly" (Deut. 1:36, Josh. 14:8). God had given them a mission, and they were wholehearted enough to take it on.

Joshua became the leader of Israel after the death of Moses. Caleb, a mighty warrior into his old age, was granted a large parcel of land in Judea after the land was conquered.

Here's another illustration. When David was planning and providing for his son Solomon to build a temple to the Lord in Jerusalem, the people of Israel responded so generously that David had to *tell them to stop giving*! There was no more room to store the riches coming in, "for they had given freely and *wholeheartedly* to the Lord" (1 Chron. 29:9, emphasis added). David rejoiced. What leader wouldn't rejoice at that kind of response to a building fund drive? These worshippers were all in on creating a sacred space to honor God.

Before his death, the following is part of David's instruction to Solomon:

> "And you, my son Solomon, acknowledge the God of your father, and serve him with *wholehearted* devotion and with a willing mind, for the Lord searches every heart and understands every desire and every thought. If you seek

him, he will be found by you; but if you forsake him, he will reject you forever. Consider now, for the Lord has chosen you to build a house as the sanctuary. Be strong and do the work." (1 Chron. 28:9–10, emphasis added)

Later, at the dedication of the completed temple, Solomon cries out,

"Lord, the God of Israel, there is no God like you in heaven above or on earth below—you who keep your covenant of love with your servants who continue *wholeheartedly* in your way." (1 Kings 8:23, emphasis added)

Solomon knew that the key to the kingdom is wholehearted devotion to the God who makes impossible things possible.

What is true of kings is also true of servants. And who are we? I can't answer for you, but I am pleased to see myself as a servant. And "as for me and my household, we will *serve* the Lord" (Josh. 24:15, emphasis added).

Interestingly, in Ephesians 6, Paul refers to wholeheartedness when addressing those who serve earthly masters. He exhorted them to serve with "respect and fear, and with sincerity of heart, just as you would obey Christ" (v. 5). Then, to amplify this idea, he pleads:

Serve wholeheartedly, as if you were serving the Lord, not people, because you know that the Lord will reward each one for whatever good they do. (Eph. 6:5–8)

Everything we do, we dedicate to him. We don't do it only to receive a reward, but it helps to know that we will be rewarded for our efforts if we do not quit.

According to these passages, wholeheartedness has everything to do with work! But it is not limited to certain types of work. It is applicable to:

Building…cleaning…designing…caring…feeding… managing…leading…painting…sweeping…selling…

giving…counseling…writing…studying…teaching…
mentoring…praying…

Other ___________________ What do you write here?

These thoughts and Scriptures about wholehearted living challenge us with the questions: Are we willing to do our work until the end? Will we put our hand to the plow and not look back? (Luke 9:62.)

This is not about salvation. Salvation is a redemptive work of God's grace in the heart of anyone who puts faith and trust in the Savior. It is about allowing the Lord to inspire wholehearted feats of strength, courage, and sacrifice in his name.

It is about reaching for the prize, like those contestants on AGT. But our prize is so much better than a million dollars and the applause of people. It is union with the fiery, passionate heart of the God of the universe, and hearing the applause of heaven.

"Consider now, for the Lord has chosen you…. Be strong and do the work" (1 Chron. 28:10).

CONNECTED

I love being a musician and worship leader. I love playing my guitar before the Lord because I know that the sound it produces changes the spiritual atmosphere. And in that changed atmosphere, I see the Lord touch peoples' hearts.

Many guitar players are gifted with technology, but all the pedals and wires, switches, inputs, and outputs—not my thing. Cables especially; I'm always tripping over or getting tangled up in them. When I led worship up in Ohio, before leaving the platform after a practice or service, I would wait for my husband to come and untangle me before I could safely walk away.

For this reason, I always appreciate those who have a gift for running sound and making sure equipment is working as it should and helping the musicians flow in their anointings.

One morning, as I was setting up and plugging in, getting ready to run through our songs for the service, I hit a snag. The tuner wouldn't give me a reading and my in-ear monitors weren't feeding me my guitar sound. But I could hear my voice in my vocal microphone.

The worship pastor and soundman and I looked at the monitor panel, the soundboard, and the guitar settings and didn't see anything out of place. And then, we saw that my input cable was not securely connected to the pedal board that was connected to the system.

What occurred to me in that moment was a concept I learned called Occam's razor. Occam was a philosopher and theologian known for the brilliant idea that the simplest explanation is usually the correct one.

Or at least, it should be considered, and not eliminated just because it seems too simple. The answer in this case was simple: I wasn't getting any power because I was not fully connected to the source.

The analogy to spiritual power is pretty obvious. If there is no connection at all, there is no power at all. That's clear. Without the infilling of the Holy Spirit that connects us to the source of all truth, wisdom, and goodness, however we might try to make an impact on the spiritual realm, we can't do it. Jesus said that if we are not integrally attached to him, "abiding in the vine," we can do nothing (John 15). We can do nothing in his name that is, or for his kingdom. The stuff that matters the most.

Jesus said, "I tell you the truth, no one can enter the kingdom of God unless they are born of water and the Spirit. Flesh gives birth to flesh, but the Spirit gives birth to spirit. You should not be surprised at my saying, 'You must be born again'" (John 3:5). We don't have access to spiritual power until we become born again of the Spirit.

We can also connect in part, but not as completely as we need to be, like I was this morning. The tuner was receiving a signal, but it was a garbled message, and the tuner became confused and unstable. I could hear only part of the mix.

If we are not careful, we can find ourselves with one ear tuned to the good news of the Lord and the other ear tuned to the endless flow of bad news from the world. It can become difficult and confusing to discern the truth, and without the truth, we can't operate in full spiritual power. We must worship him "in Spirit *and* in truth" (John 4:24, emphasis added), and to do this we must remove the impediments to our solid, reliable connection with him.

I'm glad we were able to quickly solve our little technical glitch and get on with the ministry. Often in the spiritual realm, it is also a simple answer:

> My heart says of you, "Seek his face!"
> Your face, Lord, I will seek. (Ps. 27:8)

SALTY

In a discourse about the cost of being a disciple, Jesus asks his audience rhetorically, "Salt is good, but if it loses its saltiness, how can you make it salty again?" He teaches, "Have salt in yourselves, and be at peace with each other" (Mark 9:50). In Luke he adds that if salt loses its saltiness, "it is fit neither for the soil nor for the manure pile; it is thrown out" (14:34–35). In the Sermon on the Mount, he calls his disciples "the salt of the earth" (Matt. 5:13). He implies that true disciples are salty and warns that when disciples become "unsalty" they become useless in his kingdom.

Salt served several essential functions in the ancient world of the Israelites. Households used it in the ways that we use it—primarily as flavoring for our foods. Paul uses an analogy of saltiness when he admonishes the Colossians, "Be wise in the way you act toward outsiders; make the most of every opportunity. Let your conversation be always full of grace, *seasoned with salt*, so that you may know how to answer everyone" (4:5–6, emphasis added). Our conversation should never be bland or flavorless when we speak of Jesus the Messiah.

When we serve a meal to someone, we make sure it has enough flavor to make it palatable. Salt is usually the first choice because it is so versatile and has a way of lifting and improving the other flavors in the food. Applying this metaphor, when we are sharing gospel truths, our presentation must be savory. Let our teaching and preaching lift the truth of Jesus so it can be received and consumed with joy.

Salt has great value as a preservative in places without refrigerators and freezers. Salt keeps perishable foods from going bad. If we are plenty salty, rot and decay won't set into our souls. Our saltiness ensures our goodness and extends our "shelf life." This means that our testimony has lasting value to others as well.

Israel added salt to their sacrificial grain and burnt offerings according to the commandments of the Law. Salt symbolized the everlasting covenant with God (Num. 18:19; 2 Chr. 13:5). If we are salty in our corporate worship, we remind each other of our family relationship to God and one another. The bread we share in communion contains salt, symbolizing our covenantal relationships in God's kingdom.

Finally, salt can be used as a weapon against the enemy. Salt was poured over conquered land to destroy its fruitfulness and signal total dominance (see Judg. 9:45, Job 39:6).[1] Isn't it fascinating that the same God-given substance that brings flavor and goodness in one context brings barrenness and destruction in another?

When it comes to our words and our testimony of Jesus, we are to be flavorful and bring the preserving power of his gospel to those in need of preservation. As worshippers, we remember the sacred salt covenant that saves and keeps us for heaven's use. This has the added effect of ruining the enemy's power to harm us!

Stay salty, my friends!

I think I'll have a pretzel.

---

1. Keith A. Burton, s.v. "Salt," *Eerdmans Dictionary of the Bible* (Accordance Bible Software), ed. David Noel Freedman, 1153.

WARM

Jesus's prophecies of the dramatic end of the age contain an implied warning for his people to *stay warm*.

> "At that time many will turn away from the faith and will betray and hate each other, and many false prophets will appear and deceive many people. Because of the increase of wickedness, *the love of most will grow cold,* but the one who stands firm to the end will be saved." (Matt. 24:10–13, emphasis added)

The implication of this part of Jesus's prophecy is that we as his followers are not to allow our hearts to grow cold, no matter how frigid the environments that surround us. We are to stay warm. Warm toward the Father, Son, and Holy Spirit; warm toward the people in our lives; and warm—I dare say, even *hot*—in our passion for justice and mercy.

Before going further, allow me to clarify something. Jesus warned the churches in Revelation against *lukewarmness*:

> "I know your deeds, that you are neither cold (invigorating, refreshing) nor hot (healing, therapeutic); I wish that you were cold or hot." (Rev. 3:15 AMP)

So, I'm not talking about lukewarmness, but the right kind and level of warmth, the right temperature. Warm like the first cup of coffee or tea in the morning that goes down and fills our innards with comfort and readies us for the day. When coffee sits too long and starts to cool, it's not very appetizing.

When reading the exposition of prophesied events in Matthew 24, it is tempting to focus on the timing and not the meaning of these events. Any time Jesus's disciples tried to get him to reveal the times and seasons for cataclysmic future events to occur, Jesus never took the bait. He always clarified that though the Father had given him all authority, this didn't extend to the timing of things. Only the Father knows the timetable and holds the master plan, which Jesus will execute in his authority as King of kings and Lord of lords. Therefore, even if we are convinced that the extended prophecy of end-time events in Matthew 24 (of which I've only quoted a small portion) corresponds with what we are seeing in the news or on social media, we can't be sure.

Jesus says in various places that rather than being concerned with time, we need to be concerned with our hearts, our behaviors, and our actions. But especially our hearts, because "out of the heart flow all of the issues of life" (Prov. 4:23, NKJV). We may be the generation who will see the end of this present system of things, and maybe not. But either way, we will be accountable for the condition of our hearts and how we live accordingly.

We must not grow cold. What are signs of growing cold? Lack of zeal for the Word of God for an extended time. Wickedness, unforgiveness, and injustice toward the poor, widows, and orphans all indicate hearts that are growing cold. Refusal to submit to authorities that God has ordained can freeze us out. Disconnection from his church and living in isolation have a chilling effect.

Like the charcoal briquette that is scattered too far from the center of the flame will quickly grow cold and useless, we will shiver with cold if we move away from our spiritual family. We must stay close to our brothers and sisters, however challenging this may be at times. Our survival truly depends on it.

We are to extend warmth even to our enemies. Paul exhorts us in Romans not to seek vengeance upon our enemies. On the contrary:

"If your enemy is hungry, feed him; if he is thirsty, give him something to drink. In doing this, you will heap burning coals on his head" (Rom. 12:20).

This Scripture implies that by staying warm toward those who are cold toward us, our warmth will transfer to them and convict their hearts. It is hard to stay mad at someone who insists on showing grace, love, and forgiveness from a warm heart.

This may be a challenging concept for us, especially if we focus only on a belief that everything, that everything in the church and the world is just going to get worse and worse, and there's little to be done about it. As Bill Johnson points out in his brilliant *When Heaven Invades Earth: A Practical Guide to a Life of Miracles*, this belief system requires no faith and no courage. And, I would add, no warmth. This philosophy can cause the most noble of hearts to grow cold.

Instead, we can embrace our mission to serve Christ by serving others and keep the heat on in our own hearts each day. We do this through consistent time in Scripture, through fervent prayer, through regular fellowship, through ministering gifts of healing and deliverance, and through giving generously. By all of these means we keep ourselves close to the flame and have an abundance of warmth to share with others.

BOLD

I came to faith in Christ when I was a twenty-something fledgling musician and undergraduate in New York City. When I ventured out, I would sling my guitar over the shoulder of my thrift-shop wool coat, throw a dashing fedora on my head, and act as tough and well defended as a five-foot, red-headed girl can act on the streets of the mean city.

I told my parents and others who were worried about my safety that if I was going to live in New York, I was not going to live afraid. It would be fair to say that denial was my most reliable defense mechanism at that time in my life.

Then I fell in love with Jesus and the Word of God. I memorized the Twenty-third Psalm. I remember occasions when I was walking through particularly dodgy neighborhoods and I would recite that psalm aloud over and over: *Yea, though I walk through the valley of the shadow of death, I shall fear no evil. Thy rod and thy staff they comfort me.*

Now as I stand on the brink of senior-hood, I still refuse to live afraid. I'm inspired in this conviction by Peter the apostle and his progression from fear and confusion to great boldness and power in ministry. Peter started out as a normal, natural man, a fisherman. He responded to Jesus's blunt invitation to leave his trade and become a fisher of men. He became a follower, and then one of the Twelve, and then one of Jesus's closest friends and confidants.

Peter was astonished by Jesus's teaching and his miracles, and he was often quite afraid of the phenomenal events that were unfolding.

But he was a leader, and because of his impetuous personality style he was the one to speak up when the disciples had questions they were afraid to ask. But this doesn't change the fact that often Peter was quite befuddled, confused, and afraid about what the future might bring.

All of this changed after the resurrection of Christ and the day of Pentecost. Peter became convinced of things about which he formerly doubted. His faith was secure. He was filled with the Spirit and spoke the word with reckless boldness. He counted it a joy to suffer for the name of Christ. He didn't worry about being jailed, flogged, falsely accused, or even killed. He was absolutely stuck on being a witness of the resurrection, advancing and guiding the church, and fulfilling the commission entrusted to him.

If we are Christians, we, like Peter, are filled with the Holy Spirit. We have a choice. We can cower in fear of viruses, storms, or financial downturns. We can "social distance" ourselves right out of our usefulness as ministers of the gospel. Or we can be like Peter and become bold as lions. We can stay glued to the truths of the gospel and find our security and peace in the Rock of Ages.

To quote Paul, Peter's very bold brother in Christ, "If we live, we live to the Lord; and if we die, we die to the Lord. So, whether we live or die we belong to the Lord" (Rom. 14:8). We belong to the Lord. He has us covered in every way. He is our comprehensive insurance policy.

We all must die of something if we go before Jesus returns. Some of us will be lucky enough to live to a good old age and die peacefully in our sleep. Some of us will perish because of diseases or accidents, or violence, or viruses that appear out of nowhere.

I believe we should wash our hands, pay attention to our surroundings, and be cautious and considerate of the welfare of those around us. But I will never believe in living afraid. Let us ask the Lord to make us bold and courageous.

> Have I not commanded you? Be strong and courageous.
> Do not be afraid; do not be discouraged, for the Lord
> your God will be with you wherever you go. (Josh. 1:9)

3

IN PARABLES & METAPHORS

*For since the creation of the world God's invisible qualities
his eternal power and divine nature
have been clearly seen, being understood
from what has been made...*

ROMANS 1:20

Metaphor is a powerful communication tool. Jesus showed his love for metaphors by filling his teachings with imagery, parables, and object lessons. Parables and metaphors convey complex principles and truths with immediacy and relevance to the intended audience.

The Old Testament is also replete with metaphors, throughout all genres. The prophets and psalmists were especially generous with metaphors that tell the story of Yahweh in creation, rescue, redemption, judgment, and salvation. He is a rock, a king, a stronghold, a fountain, a high tower, a shepherd, and so much more. The manifold glories and graces of God in both testaments defy everyday language. Those who speak for him must turn to poetry and story to capture even a small concept of who he is.

Scripture also reveals through metaphor aspects of our identity and purpose as people of faith. We are salt and light, thirsty like the deer, drinking from fountains, not cisterns, wearing or removing veils of deception. The Holy Spirit appropriately inspires the writers of Scripture with word pictures that bypass our intellects and aim directly at our imaginations and experiences.

The essays in this chapter are reflections on some of my favorite metaphors in Scripture. They have spoken to me very personally as I've sought greater intimacy with God, obedience to his Word, and holiness in my heart and life.

AS THE DEER

In 2021 my husband and I moved to the beautiful Hill Country of central Texas. One of the true blessings is looking out the back windows of our home and seeing deer grazing. Sometimes there are just one or two, sometimes a half dozen or more. We delight that we are living so closely and harmoniously with wild things–songbirds, squirrels, and these deer that are among the loveliest of God's created things.

My husband, Rick, decided to start feeding them. At first, he thought he could do some sort of psych job on them. He thought if he fed them food especially for them, they wouldn't eat the shrubbery we are planting to beautify the place. The joke is on him, it turns out. They eat the corn he puts out, and they're also happy to eat the geraniums as salad to go with it.

He's made a ritual of it. He walks out with a red scoop of deer corn in his hand. He spreads it out on the ground and then bangs on the scoop to alert them that it's suppertime. A la Pavlov, he believes that he is conditioning the deer to come find the food when they hear the thud on the bucket. Neutral stimulus becomes conditioned stimulus.

It just might be working. Whereas they would keep a good distance away when anyone was outside, now they come into the yard and stare at us while we're standing out there.

I am not the first worshipper in history to connect with this image of thirsty deer who come looking for sustenance. The first biblical reference that leaps to the mind might be from the psalm that speaks of our longing for God:

> As the deer pants for streams of water, so my soul pants
> for you, O God. (Ps. 42:1)

This is a marvelous metaphor: the believers are like wild deer, who must spend their days seeking food and water, finding provision provision and rest once they arrive at the right source. Deer, while agile and quick-moving, are pursued and eaten by many predators, including humans. Believers are like deer in that they are often prey for the enemy.

Jeremiah lamented that Israel had stopped following God's ways and receiving his provision and protection, likening them to deer wandering without finding pasture and running from their enemies (Lam. 1:7). Like Israel, when we don't submit ourselves to his watchful care and leadership, we wander around the metaphoric wilderness searching in vain for an adequate supply of daily bread and places to hide from danger while we eat it. But when we humbly embrace our desperate need for God, we find our way into his daily care for us.

Like those deer, who were skittish and untrusting at first, we become bolder to approach and ask for his help.

> Let us then approach the throne of grace with confidence,
> so that we may receive mercy and find grace to help us in
> our time of need. (Heb. 4:16)

Deer are swift and graceful. When we follow in Christ's footsteps, we, too, become nimble and sure-footed instead of trying to navigate on our own and stumbling through life: "The Sovereign Lord is my strength! He will make me as surefooted as a deer and bring me safely over the mountains" (Hab. 3:19, NLT).

One more biblical image related to deer that brings the analogy to another level. This is Isaiah's prophetic promise to those who seek the Lord wholeheartedly:

> Then will the eyes of the blind be opened and the
> ears of the deaf unstopped.

Then will the lame leap like a deer, and the mute
     tongue shout for joy.
Water will gush forth in the wilderness and streams in
     the desert.
The burning sand will become a pool, the thirsty
     ground bubbling springs.
In the haunts where jackals once lay, grass and reeds
     and papyrus will grow. (Isaiah 35:5–7)

We are given the opportunity to live in God's order, a spiritual and natural habitat where we can truly flourish and be unafraid. There is healing, new sight, new sound, restored movement and speech. We live near flowing springs and streams, no longer afraid of monsters in the night.

Praise the Lord for his wonderful gifts of goodness, mercy, and tender care.

As the Deer, photo by Ruth Stitt, 2021.

BROKEN CISTERNS
OR LIVING WATER

Tim Keller has described prayer as "intimacy with the infinite." Yes, the majestic, infinite God stoops down to hear the cries of his creatures. He comes near. In fact, he comes inside. Intimacy: Into-me-you-see, O Lord.

We are connected in Christ to the mystery of the infinite and the eternal. This is something difficult to grasp while in these mortal bodies. The Preacher of Ecclesiastes exclaimed:

> I have seen the burden God has laid on the human race.
> He has made everything beautiful in its time. He has also
> set eternity in the human heart; yet no one can fathom
> what God has done from beginning to end. (3:10–11)

No one can fathom God's depths. Throughout history, humans have denied this because of pride. Because Adam and Eve ate of the wrong tree, they foolishly thought they had become like God.

We still pay the price. One way that we pay the price is in our tendency to try to make the infinite finite and the eternal temporal. The prophet Jeremiah lamented over this in the name of the Lord, employing vivid metaphor:

> "My people have committed two evils: They have forsaken
> Me, the fountain of living waters, and hewn themselves

cisterns—broken cisterns that can hold no water." (Jer. 2:13, NKJV)

Instead of going to the infinite source of all life, truth, and righteousness, we choose religion, idolatry, or human wisdom over simple trust in and obedience to God's Word. We think we can tame, explain, capture the living Lord of the universe for our own purposes and find peace and satisfaction in this.

This is likened to making cisterns. Though limited in capacity, cisterns can be useful if they are intact. But the Lord tells us that these cisterns we make are not. They are useless in the end because they leak. We are always anxious that our supply will dribble away.

Jesus uses similar imagery twice in the gospel of John. To the Samaritan woman at the well, debating with him about religion, Jesus urges, "If you knew the gift of God, and who it is who says to you, 'Give Me a drink,' you would have asked Him, and He would have given you living water" (4:10). In other words, if you knew the God of infinite supply, you wouldn't be asking me for a little bucketful!

> "Everyone who drinks this water will be thirsty again, but
> whoever drinks the water I give him will never thirst.
> Indeed, the water I give him will become in him a spring
> of water welling up to eternal life." (John 4:14)

In another account, Jesus cries out to the people at the feast in Jerusalem,

> "If anyone is thirsty, let him come to Me and drink. Who-
> ever believes in Me, as the Scripture has said, streams of
> living water will flow from within him" (John 7:38).

Jesus speaks the language of rivers and fountains. He isn't interested in cisterns. He is the Lord of the infinite supply. He is the God of eternity. He is clothed in everlasting light, and his ways are past finding out (Job 36:26).

One day we will understand more fully what it means to become one with the infinite and will enjoy eternal communion with him. We will see beyond the blurriness of the looking glass. We won't try to satisfy ourselves with little sips out of our broken cisterns. We will stand overwhelmed and overcome by the gushing beauty and mystery of our holy God.

THE POTTER
AND HIS POTS

A chief biblical metaphor portrays God as a potter who sometimes forms pots from fresh clay, and sometimes from broken pieces that he reclaims. The metaphor appears first in the Psalms, several times in Isaiah and Jeremiah, and in three New Testament passages. We are pots fashioned by the hands of a Master Potter.

The prophets use the metaphor to emphasize the audacity of human beings who disrespect the creative actions of God, and think they are more important and powerful than they are. Isaiah speaks of "those who go to great depths to hide their plans from the Lord… as if the potter were thought to be like the clay!" He asks rhetorically, "Shall what is formed say to the one who formed it, 'You did not make me?' Can the pot say to the potter, 'You know nothing?'" (Isa. 29:15–17).

Isaiah returns to this theme sixteen chapters later, crying, "Woe to those who quarrel with their Maker, those who are nothing but potsherds among the potsherds on the ground. Does the clay say to the potter, 'What are you making?' Does your work say, 'The potter has no hands'?" (Isa. 45:9). Then, Isaiah answers himself: "Yet you, Lord, are our Father. We are the clay; you are the potter; we are all the work of your hand" (Isa. 64:8).

In Romans 9, Paul quotes these verses to prove the point that God decides what to do and what to impart to the many different kinds of pots he has created. We dare not question him on this as though we are smarter than he, or as though he lacks the power or wisdom to rule and reign over his creation.

Throughout human and biblical history, human beings in every generation challenge the artistry of God in their lives and circumstances. They think thoughts and pursue exploits that challenge his sovereignty and authority as Creator. They use their bodies in ways that bodies were never meant to be used, sexually and violently. They use political, economic, or demonic power to oppress others far outside of the will of God.

In Psalm 2:9, the psalmist reminds his audience that when the leaders of nations exalt themselves above the knowledge of God, God is able to "dash them to pieces like pottery." It doesn't take a lot of strength for a person to smash a clay pot. Think of what the omnipotent Lord of the universe can do if he chooses to. But our God loves mercy. We rest on this rock of truth as children of God, and as we minister to broken people.

Jeremiah's book contains one of the best-known references to the Potter and his mercy toward his broken pots. Jeremiah travels to the potter's house to learn the lesson God has for him there. As he observes the potter at the wheel, he notices that "the pot he was shaping from the clay was marred in his hands; so, the potter formed it into another pot, shaping it as seemed best to him" (Jer. 18–4).

Added to the other passages about pots and potters, this one tells us that God is interested in picking up broken pieces and forming something new "as seems best to him." He is not scared off by our marred nature. He is perfectly able to make a new, more beautiful, more functional, more pleasing pot out of shattered shards.

How great is the creative, life-restoring goodness of God! If he promised to do this restoration work for the fractured nation of Israel, he can do it also in his church. Paul writes to Timothy,

> In a large house there are articles not only of gold and silver, but also of wood and clay; some are for special purposes and some for common use. Those who cleanse themselves from the latter will be instruments for special

purposes, made holy, useful to the Master and prepared to do any good work. (2 Tim. 2:20–21)

As Christ-followers, we are vessels in God's exceptionally large house, his kingdom. He knows where to find us, and he knows how to utilize each of us for distinct purposes. He even has a personal development plan. If we desire to be made holy and most useful, there is a path to that goal: to allow him to cleanse us, sanctify us.

I know some brothers and sisters in the Lord who stay positioned very close to the Master's hand. He can reach for them easily and use them to accomplish his purposes. I learn from them as I desire to move closer and closer to the throne, to always be within his reach.

He is working on all of us. We just need to stay on the wheel, and not jump from his hands while he is still at work.

Hands of a Person Shaping a Clay Pot, photo by Vansh Sharma.

MIXTURES

There are several odd prohibitions in Deuteronomy 22 against mixing things. God forbids men dressing like women or women dressing like men, obscuring the distinction between the sexes. Israelites were forbidden to plant two crops in the same field, for example, planting beans in the rows between grapevines. If they did plant two crops, they could only use the produce from one of them, so what would be the point? They were not to yoke together an ox with a different animal like a donkey. They were not to wear wool and linen in the same outfit. A bit puzzling.

One commentary suggests that these prohibitions point back to Genesis, where God created everything "after its kind." God didn't perform an experiment in which he mashed together different parts of one organism to create another and watch to see how it turned out. He made the elephant, the fox, the hummingbird, the tortoise, the ladybug—all unique and complete, unique in their form, function, and purpose. He must enjoy the unmistakable uniqueness and variety of millions of creatures each fashioned into a distinct form.

That makes sense. Even so, isn't this a curious set of regulations? Could it be that there is meaning here for us? Of course, everything in God's book is relevant to the believer. As Paul reminds us, "For everything that was written in the past was written to teach us, so that through the endurance taught in the Scriptures and the encouragement they provide we might have hope" (Rom. 15:4).

The mixing of livestock has a simple application to human relationships. We know from New Testament Scripture that believers are not to become "unequally yoked" to unbelievers (2 Cor. 6:14, KJV). This applies to choosing a mate. There are many tales about Christian men and women who marry unbelievers, thinking that they will lead their spouse to the Lord after they are married. Sometimes this works out, praise God. But often it results in deep sorrow, frustration, and loneliness, for either or both partners. The life of Christian discipleship is difficult enough with a like-minded partner. It is inadvisable, according to Scripture—and common sense—to add the complication of pairing a believer with an unbeliever. How can they pull together in the same direction when they are not united in their view of God, the world, ultimate reality, even the purposes of marriage itself?

This principle can also be applied to business or financial partnerships. Sometimes, while navigating in the business world, we realize that we are mixing alliances with two incompatible kingdoms, with a foot in each. The Lord tells us to choose which one we will serve—the kingdom of God or the world's systems. If we choose to plant both feet firmly in the kingdom of God, we may have fewer clients and make less money overall. But our hearts will be clean, undivided, and free. Jesus warns us not to stay yoked to worldly systems that wear us out. He issues the invitation:

> "Come to me, all you who are weary and burdened, and I will give you rest. Take my *yoke* upon you and learn from me, for I am gentle and humble in heart, and you will find rest for your souls. For my *yoke* is easy and my burden is light." (Matt. 11:28–30, emphasis added)

We can't wear two yokes. If we are wearing a yoke of world-weariness, we must shed that yoke and take on the gentle, peaceable yoke of the rabbi Jesus. When we do, we begin pulling in rhythm with him, matching his stride, no longer distracted by the doctrines and philosophies of the world. The double-minded person is unstable (James 1:8), having a confused, mixed-up mind and prayer life. Jesus says we can be at peace.

Moving through the passage, the issues of mixing of crops and fabrics are less clear. One application is that God calls individuals to produce a specific type of fruit. When we exert effort in too many directions at once, we may not be as fruitful as we would be if we devoted those efforts to only one. It may not be what this Scripture is intended to convey, but it points to a truth and validates our experience. When our ministry efforts are too scattered, our harvest may be stunted. This could suggest that we should find a crop and a row, and diligently sow and reap there. As a minister friend tells me, "I try to stay in my own lane."

And what about the clothing God's people wear? How we dress and present ourselves is an aspect of holiness, being set apart for the Lord, and looking like we are his. This can be tricky. Do we ask Jesus if he's pleased with our appearance as we venture out each day?

We are not bound by the laws of ancient Israel, so I trust that Jesus doesn't mind if we wear a wool- and cotton-blend blazer, or a gold ring next to a silver ring, or an outfit that is not distinctly masculine or feminine. But he does care that our appearance, countenance, behavior, and speech all match. We should look different in a way that reminds people of him.

What are we allowed to mix? Love, joy, peace, patience, kindness, goodness, faithfulness, gentleness, and self-control. And "the law is not against these things" (Gal. 5:25).

BREAD FROM HEAVEN

The extended narrative of Israel's deliverance from Egyptian slavery and her journey through the wilderness is a deep, rich vein of truth to mine and apply. This includes the story of the manna found in Exodus 16.

The introduction of manna takes place merely a month after the Hebrew slaves' hasty flight from Egypt, and it unfortunately begins with their complaining. After witnessing ten displays of God's fearsome power and a series of miraculous interventions on their behalf, the "whole community of Israel" could only murmur and gripe about their traveling conditions and, particularly, the perceived scarcity of food and water. Some even longed to return to Egypt, where at least there was plenty to eat.

When Moses conveyed their case to the Lord, God assured Moses that their complaints were against himself, and not against Moses or his brother Aaron. This is my first point of application to our own journey as Christ-followers. When we have been delivered from slavery—which we all have been when we are born again—and we complain about our circumstances, we must realize that we are complaining against the Lord. He is our Father, and we are his children. He has committed himself to our care.

When things become difficult, we are tempted to return to our sin addiction (our Egypt). We didn't enjoy the oppression of sin, but at least it feels familiar. A journey through the wilderness toward the Promised Land is full of the unknown, but it leads to a land of freedom and abundance. When we complain, we are complaining about the very provision of God.

> Then the Lord said to Moses, "Look, I'm going to rain down food from heaven for you." (v. 4, NLT)

Here was the Lord's promise to provide, but it came with a test. He would daily rain it down, and they would daily pick it up *according to his specific instruction.* They were to only gather two quarts for each person per day, and no more. On the sixth day they were to gather twice as much, so they could have a Sabbath rest on the seventh day and not have to gather food. In this way, no one could hoard food, and no one would lack adequate food. All would have "just enough."

The Israelites had a terrible time with these simple tests of obedience. They picked up extra, only to find the next morning that the leftover manna was full of maggots and had a rotten smell. On the sixth day, they gathered twice as much, as instructed, but didn't understand why there was twice as much to gather, even though they had been told the reason. On the Sabbath, some of them went out to gather, and wouldn't you know, there was no manna to be found. The whole "food from heaven" concept eluded them.

> The Israelites were puzzled when they saw it. "What is it?" they asked each other. They had no idea what it was. (v. 15, NLT; the word *manna* means, "What is it?")

This brings us to application number two. As we make our way through the wilderness of the world, God makes provision for us. It looks different from what we fed on before he rescued us. Our daily bread falls like dew on the grass—to nourish our bodies and our souls, to heal our hearts and enlighten our understanding. We are not to get our needs met in the old ways, but according to the instruction he provides in his book.

We don't get ahead or fall behind in our obedience. We are not to be led by fear of lack or by greed. And we are to rest when God says to rest. When they saved the Friday leftovers to eat on Saturday, "the leftover food was wholesome and good, without maggots or odor" (v. 25, NLT). If we do things God's way, there is no blight, no infestation, no stink upon our lives. Bottom line, this is the test: Do we trust God?

Moses collected a sample of manna to keep inside the ark of the covenant so that "later generations will be able to see the food I gave you in the wilderness when I set you free from Egypt" (v. 32, NLT). The Lord rained down manna every day (except the Sabbath days) for the next forty years, and it sustained Israel until they were able to plant crops in the land of Israel, the land of milk and honey.

This brings us to application number three. As we journey with God, we are to remember and relate to all generations our testimony of the Lord's rescue. We are to celebrate and marvel at the miracles he has done, including his heaven-sent provision. We tell people about receiving bread from heaven.

THE VEIL

One of the metaphors that appears in both the Old and New Testaments is that of the veil. As with all biblical metaphors, this reference to a mundane object in the natural points us to truths about spiritual reality.

We know that a veil covers a bride's face until she approaches her waiting husband-to-be at the altar. He has the honor of "uncovering" her in that moment to reveal her beauty, her identity, and her vulnerability. So important is the heavenly transaction of a wedding covenant that all parties present confirm with the lifting of the veil the identity of the bride being joined to the groom, reinforced by the verbal confirmation of the bride's father. (We see in Jacob's story the danger of having the bride's identity veiled by darkness on the wedding night. Jacob unknowingly consummated a marriage to the "wrong" woman.) A veil in this case is meant to conceal identity until it is removed for dramatic effect, and then the bride makes her vows with an unveiled, radiant face.

Another reference is made to a veil in 2 Corinthians 3:12–16, where Paul recalls the Exodus 34 story of Moses covering his face with a veil because of the brightness of the glory of the Lord radiating from him:

> We are not like Moses, who would put a *veil* over his face to prevent the Israelites from seeing the end of what was passing away. [14] But their minds were made dull, for to this day the same *veil* remains when the old covenant is read. It has not been removed, because only in Christ is

it taken away. Even to this day when Moses is read, a *veil* covers their hearts. But whenever anyone turns to the Lord, the *veil* is taken away. (emphasis added)

Moses had been alone on the mountain with the Lord, transcribing the Ten Commandments on stone tablets. Being in the presence of the Lord made his face radiant, and the people—even his own brother—were afraid of this transformed Moses. He put a veil over his face while sharing God's words with the people. Then, when he was ready to climb up the hill and do another round with the Lord, he took the veil off. He wasn't afraid to approach the Lord with his face uncovered. I imagine he enjoyed being covered in the glory and glow of the Almighty!

Paul uses this veil imagery to describe his own Jewish contemporaries who had rejected Yeshua and the New Covenant. Their very minds were covered with a veil, so that they could not comprehend the surpassing glory revealed in the New Covenant, the covenant of the Spirit, the covenant of freedom:

> Now the Lord is the Spirit, and where the Spirit of the Lord is, there is freedom. And we all, who with *unveiled faces* contemplate the Lord's glory, are being transformed into his image with ever-increasing glory, which comes from the Lord, who is the Spirit. (vv. 17–18, emphasis added)

Paul attributes blame for the persistent blindness produced by the veil not to the unbeliever, but to the "god of this age." It is Satan, the father of lies, who obscures the truth (2 Cor. 4:4). Paul's urgent mission—and ours, if we choose to accept it—is to declare Christ and bring the light and freedom he offers. Only in Christ is the veil taken away.

When Christ enters, people walking in darkness begin to see reality with an unveiled face, and all looks different! All is made new. Like Moses, the believer boldly comes into the Lord's presence and begins to radiate his Spirit, his power, his light, his love. A new identity in him is radiated into the world. Like the bride on her wedding day, we gaze lovingly into the face of our perfect bridegroom and bask in our shared light.

> Those who look to him are radiant; their faces are never covered with shame. (Ps. 34:5)

SEED TIME
AND HARVEST

The amazing and beautiful story of Jesus's encounter with the Samaritan woman in John 4 includes an aside, in which Jesus speaks to his disciples about harvest. When the woman abruptly runs off to call her neighbors out to meet the extraordinary man Jesus, the Messiah, he uses the pause to point out the ripeness of the harvest all around them and the need for workers. He asks,

> 'Don't you have a saying, 'It's still four months until harvest'? I tell you, open your eyes and look at the fields! They are ripe for harvest. Even now the one who reaps draws a wage and harvests a crop for eternal life, so that the sower and the reaper may be glad together. Thus, the saying 'One sows and another reaps' is true. I sent you to reap what you have not worked for. Others have done the hard work, and you have reaped the benefits of their labor." (John 4:35–38)

Because they lived in an agrarian society, Jesus often used metaphors from agriculture to teach his disciples. His parables are rich with the vocabulary of farming—seeds, roots, weeds, watering, cultivating, sowing, reaping, and harvest. Paul, James, and John followed suit in their writings. There is no biblical metaphor that better or as frequently captures the essence of the kingdom of God than planting, watering, and producing a harvest. Jesus refers to the world waiting to hear the gospel as God's "harvest field" (Matt. 9:38).

Farming happens according to seasons and cycles. We understand that it works, but there is an element of mystery in how it works, as Jesus alludes to in this passage:

> "This is what the kingdom of God is like. A man scatters seed on the ground. Night and day, whether he sleeps or gets up, the seed sprouts and grows, though he does not know how. All by itself the soil produces grain—first the stalk, then the head, then the full kernel in the head. As soon as the grain is ripe, he puts the sickle to it, because the harvest has come." (Mark 4:26–29)

It appears that like many of his teachings, this one exhorts us to trust and act by faith, even when we do not fully comprehend all aspects of his instruction. Embracing mystery is part of discipleship. But we do know enough about what Jesus has called us to do, and what is our rightful part in bringing in a harvest of souls.

First, if we follow Jesus's example, we will be reckless sowers of the seeds of gospel truth. According to the parable of the sower and the seed, the sower throws out so much seed in every direction that some of it lands in places where it has no chance of taking root and growing to maturity. We are not to spare the seed by pre-judging who is good ground and who is not. We scatter it far and wide. This seed sowing is the work of evangelism.

When the seed has been sown, the soil must be watered. When the seed sprouts and the new stalk is still tender and fragile, it must be protected from intense heat and wind. If weeds start to surround the young plant, the farmer sees to it that the plant's growth is not thwarted. This husbandry is a picture of the work of discipling (Matt. 13:24–29).

Some in the kingdom are primarily evangelists, some are primarily disciplers, and most of us do some of each, and serve in other ways as well. But the glory of the harvest belongs entirely to the Lord. The apostle Paul, who was a planter and cultivator of much gospel seed, declared, "I have planted, Apollos watered; but God gave the increase" (1 Cor. 3:6–7). God's people are workers in the harvest, while God is Lord of the harvest and receives all the credit for its abundance.

Another interesting aspect of this agricultural imagery is that there are always weeds that grow amid the crop. In the parable of the wheat and the tares, Jesus teaches that the wheat (the true believers) and the tares (the unbelievers and evildoers of the world) grow up together. Just as we can't take credit for a good crop, we don't have the authority to sort out and destroy the weeds. We can't eradicate the weeds without damaging the wheat, so this must await the end of the age, when the Lord himself and his angels will separate them (Matt. 13:25–26).

When considered together, these agricultural parables teach us to sow the Word generously and to watch over and care for new believers diligently. We work at these things patiently and zealously, trusting God to bring the increase of the fruits of the harvest. We have the privilege of partnering with him in the stewardship of his kingdom.

THE SEAL OF GOD

Set me as a seal upon thine heart, as a seal
upon thine arm: for love is strong as death.

Song 8:6a. kjv, emphasis added

Occasionally I will buy or be gifted a product that is ensconced in seemingly impenetrable plastic and cardboard packaging. I'll wrestle with it a little bit, but I have a low frustration tolerance for this sort of thing. Thankfully, my husband or daughter will notice, and being individuals with stronger mechanical skills, they will rescue me and extricate the object from its hard shell.

Whoever decided to package it that way wanted to ensure it got to the designated recipient clean, whole, and without signs of tampering. This is a fitting analogy for the way in which Christ-followers have been sealed by God—authenticated, protected, and marked—with no expiration date.

When the Bible was written, it was customary to use a seal, made of clay or wax, to close a letter or official document. It would often be marked with an insignia of the sender pressed into the wax by a ring or stamp. References to this type of seal are found in Deuteronomy, Nehemiah, Esther, Job, Song of Solomon, and all the major prophets.

Usually, a sealed document contained an official order by an important ruler or a written covenant between two parties. If a document was sealed in this way, it indicated authenticity and the full authority of the sender and signatory. The seal protected the document from being violated by someone other than the intended recipient.

In the New Testament, the concept and imagery of the seal are used quite a few times. Jesus proclaimed that God seals those who belong to him. The seal indicates that the believer has the unconditional guarantee of eternal life (John 6:27). The seal tells the world that an individual has received the testimony of God and believes it to be true (John 3:33). The seal marks those who belong to him.

Paul later refers to the sign of circumcision given to Abraham as a "seal of the righteousness of the faith while he was still uncircumcised. So then, he is the father of all who believe…" (Rom. 4:11). In other words, circumcision became the outward sign—or seal with God's insignia—that God had already rewarded the inward faith of Abraham. For the Spirit-filled believer, instead of an outward sign on the body, the seal is the "Holy Spirit of promise" (Eph. 1:13), eternally packaged and sealed upon the heart. (2 Cor. 1:22). It is evidence of the promise of eternal life.

This is a better sign of our covenant with God than any engagement ring or physical mark could be. This Spirit that seals also imparts and infuses the believer with holy fire and supernatural power. What a privilege it is to carry this seal of God upon our hearts! The Holy Spirit within testifies that we have been bought and paid for by the perfect blood of Jesus Christ. We are his beloved, authentically and eternally joined to him by covenant.

No one can break in and wreck us without our permission. We are enclosed and surrounded by heavenly packaging!

4

IN OUR SPIRITUAL PRACTICES

Over the twenty centuries of the Christian church, many scholars, teachers, pastors, and theologians have focused on the "how" of Christian discipleship. This practical approach helps us grow and change after we have come into the kingdom of Jesus Christ. What are the ingredients in a recipe for consistent growth in our relationship with God?

Sometimes these ingredients are called spiritual disciplines. They are ways of conducting our daily lives and devotions in accord with the Scriptures and the example of Christ. But how do we develop these disciplines without falling into rote religiosity or legalism? How do we keep our faith strong and alive?

In these essays, I explore some of the ways we practice our faith. We'll look at the importance of praise, confession, prayer, communion, and rest. We'll also see that our spiritual practices reflect much about our value system and how we stop thriving when we neglect them. Are we too surrounded by noise and busyness, and in need of solitude? Are we generous with our material wealth and with our love toward those in need?

In Christ we have been transformed. We have become spiritual creatures. We are in a process of growth wherein our bodies and souls come increasingly into agreement with the Spirit. We are disciples who welcome the Lord's discipline, that we may become more like him with each passing day.

PRAISE AS ASCENT

Having been a praise and worship leader for many years, I have been motivated to study the Bible's exhortations about offering praise to God. To comprehend the attitude of heart that God seeks in his worshippers, I come back consistently to the imagery of pilgrimage, ascent, and bowing down in the presence of the living God.

Psalms 120–134 in the Hebrew songbook are "Psalms of Ascent." These ancient travel songs collectively describe the journey starting from a land of trial and anguish and ending at Mount Zion and the sanctuary of the Lord. Before the journey begins, pilgrims lament the violence and deceit that surrounds them on every side. In desperation, they lift their eyes to the hills ahead, sensing that their help derives from that holy place (Ps. 121:2). They remember who they are and begin crying out to the God of their nation.

The throngs ascending to Jerusalem exclaim, "I was glad when they said to me, 'Let us go to the house of the Lord!'" (122:1, NLT). It is feast time, a holy convocation to celebrate the Lord's goodness and deliverance. He has always shielded and surrounded them "as the mountains surround and protect Jerusalem" (125:2, NLT). They excitedly shout and laugh together, recalling the Lord who has restored their fortunes and done so many great things for them. Those who have sown many tears are overcome with shouts of joy! (126:5).

The closer they come to the Temple Mount, the more thankful they become—for God's blessing upon their homes, husbands and wives, children and grandchildren, their land, work, and nation. At times they pause to reflect on the bitterness of the past. This is part of the ascent: the remembrance of God's mercy and faithfulness even at the lowest places in life. They are humbled in his presence.

They come through his gates with thanksgiving and praise. They calm and quiet their souls in his presence, contented children who simply wish to enjoy the beautiful fellowship of their benevolent Father. They reach the summit, surrounded by priests, worshippers, and provisions for sacrifice.

When I picture this, I remember the day I stood at the base of the southern steps of the temple ruins in Jerusalem. It was one of the most profound and affecting moments of my trip. I was caught up in the mystery and history of this place adjacent to the Beautiful Gate where Peter and John healed the crippled man. The ruins of the mikvehs can still be seen, where worshippers bathed before ascending the steps.

But for me the most beautiful and significant thing was that the steps are of all different heights and depths, varying from seven to ten inches high and twelve to thirty-five inches deep. Our guide explained that this forced the ascending pilgrims to climb very slowly and carefully. This is the place of the "selah," a place where one pauses repeatedly in reverence, awe, and deep prayerfulness.

The throngs of visitors, tired from their journey but cleansed and ready, prayerfully climbed those ancient steps to meet their God in his holy temple. Ever since my visit, this is the image that I associate with praise. It is a journey, a climb to the highest place we know. It is intentional. It requires effort. It involves the body, soul, and spirit. It is driven by a thankful, beating heart. It is a sacrifice. It is an ascent into the realm of the holiness of Yeshua.

We do not have access to these physical steps every day to remind us. But may we ascend in the Spirit at every opportunity to praise God with clean hands and a pure heart. What a privilege to bring ourselves into a daily encounter with our most worthy Lord and Savior!

Southern Steps of the temple in Jerusalem (public domain photo)

CONFESSION AND
THE PURE IN HEART

God gave us a way to stay forgiven, clean, pure, and righteous. It's called confession. It's ironic that our words, which create the most trouble in our lives and relationships, also serve as the mechanism for healing and release. We are set right by our confession to God and to those we have offended or wronged.

The wise authors of the Twelve Steps of Alcoholics Anonymous recognized the importance of this when they included Step 5: "We admitted to God, to ourselves, and to another human being the exact nature of our wrongs."[1] James exhorted believers to "confess your sins to each other and pray for each other so that you may be healed" (James 5:16). Confession with repentance is the only path to forgiveness and restoration in God. The full measure of healing comes when we confess our faults to another person as well.

David wrote, "When I refused to confess my sin, I was weak and miserable, and I groaned all day long…. Finally, I confessed all my sins to you and stopped trying to hide them…and you forgave me! All my guilt is gone" (Ps. 32:3, 5, NLT). Because of his sense of relief and release, David was quick to recommend this practice to others: "Therefore, let all the godly confess their rebellion to you while there is time, that they may not drown in the floodwaters of judgment" (v. 6).

---

1. Alcoholics Anonymous World Services, Inc. 1989. *Twelve Steps and Twelve Traditions*. New York, NY: Alcoholics Anonymous World Services.

The Apostle John warns members of God's family,

> "If we claim to be without sin, we deceive ourselves and the truth is not in us. If we confess our sins, he is faithful and just and will forgive us our sins and purify us from all unrighteousness. If we claim we have not sinned, we make him out to be a liar and his word is not in us" (1 John 1:8–10). This passage notes that if we refuse to confess our wrongs, not only do we stay trapped in guilt and fear of judgment, but we are also guilty of lying, and of calling God a liar. Not a good idea.

The Word of God clearly reveals that we all sin and fall short of his glory (Rom. 3:23). What God asks of us is that we own up to it. He is ready and willing to make us right again.

Good parents know this. Our children's misbehavior is not usually what potentially damages our relationships with them. Rather, it is hiding and lying about their misdeeds that breeds mistrust, conflict, and dishonor in the family. As parents, we should always incentivize truthfulness and de-incentivize dishonesty. God does.

The most important reason to quickly confess our sins to our faithful and just God is so that we keep our hearts pure before him. David concluded Psalm 32 (above), "So rejoice in the LORD and be glad, all you who obey him! Shout for joy, all you whose hearts are pure!" (Ps. 32:11 NLT).

In the Beatitudes, Jesus taught that the pure in heart are blessed, "for they will see God" (Matt. 5:5). They are able to "ascend the hill of the LORD" to worship with "clean hands and a pure heart" (Ps. 24:3–4) and stand boldly before his throne without fear or shame. This requires confession and cleansing. This is the path that elevates us to an unhindered view of the face of God.

In my prison ministry, we often recite together this beautiful corporate prayer of confession from the *Book of Common Prayer.*

> Most merciful God,
> we confess that we have sinned against you

in thought, word, and deed,
by what we have done, and by what we have left
undone.
We have not loved you with our whole heart.
We have not loved our neighbors as ourselves.
We are truly sorry and we humbly repent.
For the sake of your Son Jesus Christ,
have mercy on us and forgive us;
that we may delight in your will,
and walk in your ways,
to the glory of your Name. Amen.
("Daily Morning Prayer: Rite Two")[1]

When we finish saying this together, there is a holy hush. A quiet joy pervades the atmosphere. We are clean again. We can see God. This is the power of confession.

1. Prayer of Confession, *The Book of Common Prayer.* New York: Seabury Press, 1979.

COMMUNION AND THE WASHING OF FEET

All four of the gospel authors include details of the Last Supper, the final Passover meal Jesus shared with his twelve closest friends and followers. This was the occasion when he established the tradition of the covenant meal we call communion.

When I read narratives in the Bible, especially in the Gospels, I like to put myself there. I like to focus on what Jesus says and does in the passage as though I am an eyewitness in the room. This requires that I suspend what I know about everything that comes after the moment at hand. I must pretend I don't know the rest of the story. I try to perceive some of what Peter or Thomas would have perceived.

In this case, they would have had certain expectations for this occasion. It was Passover, and all Jewish people knew its deep significance to their nation. They knew what foods to prepare and serve, the cups of wine needed, the history to be recounted, and the prayers and blessings to be uttered.

Passover commemorated God's deliverance of the Israelites from slavery in Egypt and was a much-anticipated time of worship, feasting, and celebration. The twelve tribes throughout the land made one of their three annual pilgrimages to Jerusalem. This is what Jesus and the disciples did, culminating with Jesus's triumphal entry on a donkey.

Matthew and Mark provide very straightforward reporting of the facts of the preparations and the dinner. Jesus blessed the bread and wine and instructed them to make it a regular practice to remember the sacrifice of his body and blood each time they would partake. Although Jesus had tried to prepare them for the reality of his torture, crucifixion, three days in the tomb, and then resurrection, they didn't quite get it. Judas's betrayal was happening before their eyes, but they couldn't make sense of it. They were in considerable denial. John states clearly that the disciples didn't understand the meaning of the Passion of Jesus until after his resurrection and ascension (12:16).

Luke's gospel adds Jesus's teaching on servanthood in the context of the Passover meal. Jesus explains that in his kingdom, unlike the kingdoms of the world, greatness is determined by humility, where the "greatest among you should be like the youngest, and the one who rules like the one who serves" (Luke 22:26). He would set the example, declaring, "I am among you as one who serves" (v. 27). He would soon serve them—and us—upon a bloody cross.

It is only in the gospel of John that we see in action, not just in words, how Jesus defines servanthood. Though we know the communion meal was instituted this same night, John does not share the details of the preparations or the bread and wine. John's focus is on Jesus washing the disciples' feet. John wants his readers to understand that Jesus, "having loved his own who were in the world, he now showed them the full extent of his love" (John 13:1).

> Jesus, knowing the suffering that awaited him, quietly rose from the table, took off his outer tunic and wrapped a towel around his waist. He used water from a basin to wash each disciple's feet, and then dried them with the towel. When finished, Jesus asked them, "Do you understand what I have done for you? You call me 'Teacher' and 'Lord,' and rightly so, for that is what I am. Now that I, your Lord and Teacher, have washed your feet, you also should wash one another's feet. I have set you an example that you should do as I have done for you…Now that you know these things, you will be blessed if you do them." (John 13: 12-15, 17)

We often forget that this scene happened on the very same night, in the same room where they ate the bread and drank the wine. Could it be that when we take communion, we are not only to remember the words of Jesus as he held bread and cup in his hand but also remember him in the towel, bowing low to wash dirty feet? Could it be that when we remember him, we must also remember that he called us to be like him in our service to one another?

Communion indicates oneness—with the Father, with the Son, with the Holy Spirit, and with one another, his own body on the earth. When we take communion, eager to celebrate and remember the Savior who paid for our salvation, Jesus wants us to be just as eager to humbly serve our brothers and sisters in his name. Knowing these things, he promises that we will be blessed in doing them.

SOLITUDE

My mom used to love solo travel. Friends and family would marvel as she hung some clothes on a pole installed in the back of her Dodge Caravan, checked out some books on tape from the library, and hit the road. She was fearless that way.

Mom also loved people more than most, so it was a bit strange that she would travel on her own. She figured if she needed conversation or connection while on her adventures, she would find it. And she did—so much so that she had friends all over the country that she met in coffee shops, at pit stops, or on sightseeing excursions. Sometimes when she set out on a trip, she happily anticipated visiting folks she had met on previous journeys and would plan her itinerary to stop in for tea and sandwiches.

I also have developed a love for solo travel. But my reason for traveling alone differs from Mom's. My life in ministry is the most gratifying and exciting one I can imagine at this time in my life. But ministry only remains a healthy and productive enterprise with rigorous self-care and conscientious spiritual discipline. I've seen that those who neglect their own physical, emotional, and spiritual health for the sake of ministry run the risk of exhaustion, burnout, and moral compromise.

My solo retreats have become a spiritual practice. It is a fast of sorts—a fast from conversation and doing. As someone whose day-to-day life is about endless engagement with people, tasks, and words, it becomes necessary to stop talking and doing for a minute.

I took my first solo retreat in January 2019 and enjoyed it so thoroughly that I decided to take myself away alone every three months or so. I choose a place with beautiful and interesting places to walk, because long walks are a must. I think, sing, read, pray, and journal a lot. My chief objective is to tune into my own internal rhythms moment by moment and connect with the Spirit.

I only do what feels right, with no external demands. I talk with God, and I listen as he talks to me. I notice all the simple and lovely details of the natural and human world around me without attaching to them. Sometimes I find myself drawn into a conversation, and I can delight in that, too, because it is spontaneous and light, an occasional parenthesis in the flow of my stream of consciousness.

In Scripture, I've been noticing the pace of life experienced by Jesus once he became famous. Because of his many miraculous healings, Jesus quickly became a celebrity in Israel. He often urged recipients of healing or deliverance to keep quiet about him; he knew that his fame would draw such crowds that ministry would become difficult. He often craved unhurried time alone with his Father, and on a few recorded occasions he did slip away.

Jesus also tried to pull his twelve disciples away to the mountains, but the crowds would find them. Jesus's compassion compelled him to meet the needs of the people before attending to his own need for rest and solitude. When his cousin John was beheaded, he was allowed no time to pray and grieve, but instead kept teaching, healing, and feeding thousands.

I'm grateful for the example of Jesus's compassionate heart for ministry. I also appreciate his acknowledgment that it is important to rest, reflect, and get recharged by intimate time alone with the Father. We must press into it sometimes because the world will not make room for it.

SABBATH KEEPING

*There remains, then, a Sabbath-rest for the people
of God, for anyone who enters God's rest also rests
from their works, just as God did from his.*

Heb. 4:9–10

We all know some people who have difficulty with the discipline of work. They don't like to work or have become discouraged enough to give up and let others take care of their needs. Those with some form of infirmity or incapacity must rely on the work of others to survive. But the bottom line is that work is a gift and a privilege. Refusing to work when we are able to is considered by most of us to be an irresponsible and selfish choice.

Actually, most people I know, myself included, do not have trouble with the discipline of work. Most of us work very hard. What we struggle with is the discipline of rest. Yes, rest is a spiritual discipline. Sabbath keeping is an ancient commandment.

Most commandments in Scripture are given because they dictate something that does not happen when we live only to serve ourselves. When we come under the covering of a holy and loving God, we desire to keep his commandments. When we do what is pleasing to him, we receive his life and wholeness. One of his commands is to rest.

Why is a Sabbath rest so essential? For lots of reasons, but they might be summed up in the notion that we need a regular reminder that he is God, and we are not. When we refuse to rest, we wind up striving to prove ourselves and our abilities. We overwork, and we have trouble saying no to extra tasks when our regular work is done. We want to feel that we are in charge, in control of our circumstances and resources. This defines us and makes us feel worthwhile.

In the movie *Chariots of Fire*, two Olympian sprinters were competing for the medal. One refused to compete on the Sabbath, even if it cost him the prize. He was secure in his identity in Christ and, though he wanted to win the race, didn't need the win to validate his worthiness. The other was relying on a ten-second sprint to tell him he was worthy of taking up space in the world.

Sabbath originates in the creation story. After each work of creation, God said it was good. When he was finished, he said it all was very good, and on the seventh day, he rested. He didn't rest because he was tired. He rested because he had finished his work. I picture him sitting back and enjoying the very good things he had set in place.

Observant Jews understand that Sabbath is not only about rest but about worship, beauty, fellowship, family, and rejoicing in God's goodness. With the lighting of the Friday evening candles, they acknowledge that the God who gave them purpose throughout the workweek now gives them rest, peace, and enjoyment. They eat savory foods and drink some wine with friends and family. They attend synagogue and hear the spoken Word of God. Husbands and wives make love, and they take time to play with their children. They sit back, as God did on the seventh day, and behold the wonder and glory of what God has done.

Do contemporary Christ-followers have less need for this discipline because we live in grace? I would argue that we need it more, because it acknowledges and celebrates that our lives rest in grace. I pray that the Lord would intervene in the lives of those of us who struggle with Sabbath keeping and help us to find rest in him.

AN EXEMPLARY PRAYER LIFE

Most Christians would agree that prayer is the central discipline in a life of faith. There are many notable examples of people of prayer in the Scriptures who help us to appreciate its importance in maintaining an intimate connection with our Lord and God.

The book of Nehemiah reveals Nehemiah's habit of praying through every circumstance. At the center of the fascinating story of the return of Jewish exiles to rebuild the ravaged city of Jerusalem is this portrait of a leader who constantly relied upon God's strength, protection, and favor. He was truly a man of prayer.

The story begins with Nehemiah hearing of the suffering and devastation of the Jewish people in their homeland. He "sat down and wept and mourned for days…fasting and praying before the God of heaven" (1:4). He spoke to Yahweh as though they had a long-standing and intimate connection.

And yet Nehemiah's tone was one of awe, reverence, and an appropriate fear of God. He interceded, confessing the sins of Israel and pleading for God's mercy. He asked God to give him favor with the Persian king so that he might be permitted to undertake a mission trip to Jerusalem. During his audience with the king, he prayed silently again, and the Lord answered. Lo and behold, "it pleased the king to send me" (2:6).

The next example occurs when Nehemiah and his construction crews encounter extreme hostility and opposition from some of the local leaders in Jerusalem. Sanballat and Tobiah were the ringleaders, taunting and threatening the Jewish builders. Nehemiah's response? "And we prayed to our God and set a guard as a protection against them day and night" (4:9, ESV). The answer of God was to "frustrate" the plan of their enemies, and "we all returned to the wall, each to his work" (4:15, ESV). Nehemiah's defensive strategy was to provide the workers with a tool in one hand, a weapon in the other, and a sword strapped to their sides.

In the next chapter, the text cites Nehemiah's godly, wise leadership when conflict arose within the Jewish population. Because of his habit of seeking the Lord's counsel at every turn, he was able to arbitrate these conflicts quickly and effectively. In response to his judiciousness, "all the assembly said 'Amen' and praised the LORD" and "did as they had promised" (5:5).

The local troublemakers continued to plot against Nehemiah and his team, seeking not only to stop the work but to destroy Nehemiah's reputation and fill him with fear. In prayer, Nehemiah expressed his trust in the Lord to administer justice and protect him from every form of harm. And thus, the work was completed "with the help of our God" (6:16).

Then another amazing God-thing happened! Ezra the priest showed up with the book of the Law. The priests and Levites begin preaching and teaching all of the adults present who could understand. (8:2). Nehemiah recognized that the Spirit of God had begun to move powerfully among the people. He was a mature believer and leader, having trained his senses through prayer. He knew how to steward and shepherd the people through the sudden revival that broke out with the hearing of the Word of God. It was a glorious time!

As is often true during revival, celebration and deep repentance occurred simultaneously amid the Israelites. Nehemiah recounted for the people the history of God's goodness and forbearance with them. In his public prayer, he reminded God, "You are a God ready to forgive, gracious and merciful, slow to anger and abounding in steadfast love" (9:17, ESV). The conviction that came to the people led them to wholeheartedly renew their covenant with Yahweh. They agreed to separate themselves from pagan nations and all idolatrous practices. They pledged "to walk in God's Law that was given by Moses the servant of God, and to observe and do all the commandments of the Lord our Lord and his rules and his statutes" (11:29). The priests and Levites were also transformed, promising, to never again neglect their duties in the house of the Lord (11:39).

Having restored order and beauty to the city and temple, Nehemiah next presided over the establishment of worship in the manner of David's tabernacle. Sacrifices, dedications, and purification rituals were instituted with the background music of two grand choirs, which could be heard from far away (13:43). This is a picture of the restoration of a place and a people. It could not have happened without the leadership and authentic prayerfulness of this extraordinary man, Nehemiah.

In summary, Nehemiah demonstrated many types of prayer on many occasions. He prayed intercessory prayers, prayers of repentance, prayers for favor and protection, prayers of trust and submission, prayers for wisdom, prayers for revival, prayers of remembrance, prayers of dedication, and prayers of consecration. His wonderful story teaches us that prayer is always necessary, and always appropriate.

There is no time when crying out to God is the wrong thing to do. It is prayer to God that sends, upholds, strengthens, and rewards God's people. And God delights to hear our prayers.

THE BEAUTIFUL LAW OF GLEANING

Many students of Scripture find aspects of the law of Moses in the Pentateuch (the first five books of the Bible) unjust, archaic, or just plain baffling. Some of the laws are almost impossible to contextualize to our modern lives and beliefs—for instance, the laws regarding ritual purification, or the harsh penalties prescribed for infractions that today barely get a mild reprimand.

Amid these difficult, perplexing commands, we find the beautiful law of gleaning. The statutes pertaining to gleaning glimmer like gemstones, oddly placed. For example, between a commandment to eat the entire remainder of a fellowship offering and the simple dictate "Do not steal" is this gem:

> "When you reap the harvest of your land, do not reap
> to the very edges of your field or gather the gleanings
> of your harvest. Do not go over your vineyard a second
> time or pick up the grapes that have fallen. Leave them
> for the poor and the foreigner. I am the Lord your God."
> (Lev. 19:9–10)

This picture of leaving fruit behind might seem to us imprudent or wasteful. Shouldn't we always seek to maximize our profits and make full use of all our resources?

Not necessarily, in God's economy. Though God commends saving, thrift, and resourcefulness, generosity matters more. God wants—he commands—that his people look beyond their own needs or profits. The priority is to provide for the needs of our own families that we are able to anticipate. But God goes beyond this, admonishing his people to intentionally leave a portion of the fruits of our labor available to a needy individual who might happen along the way. The poor person or foreigner must find something to sustain him. Boaz practiced this when he saw Ruth in his fields; he encouraged her to follow his harvesters and glean enough to sustain her and her mother-in-law, Naomi.

There's no guarantee that someone like Ruth will happen along. In the case of agricultural fruits, there's a chance that the remainders will go unclaimed and just rot on the ground or dry up on the vine. In modern, monetary terms, there's a chance that leaving money on the table could limit our bottom line. But that is not to be our concern. When we refrain from greedily grabbing up all the fruit, we are acting in obedience to the law of God, and this carries its own reward.

John the Baptist hinted at this principle and its centrality to the approaching kingdom of God. Preaching a baptism of repentance, he instructed his audiences to demonstrate their repentance through true acts of generosity, giving away extra food or clothing (Luke 3:11).

To contextualize this to the church age in which we live, the apostle Paul admonishes the believer not to steal, but to "work, doing something useful with his own hands, that he may have something to share with those in need" (Eph. 4:28). We are supposed to take care of ourselves, so we do not become a burden to others. But that is not enough. We are to be diligent in the work God has given us so that there is extra on hand to share with those who are in worse circumstances.

This also applies to nonmaterial fruits. If we learn great truth through our study or reflection on the Scriptures, or through our life experiences, we ought to be prepared to make it available to those who might "accidentally" show up in our lives. Who knows when you or I might be the person with a word for the weary, someone we had no idea was coming? Can we have such abundance of the fruit of the Spirit that we always have enough for ourselves, a supply to share with those we know and love, and even plenty to give to the one who shows up at the door uninvited?

This is the beautiful law of gleaning. It releases a spirit of freedom and generosity in those who practice it, and sustenance to those who go out to glean in the harvest fields.

The Gleaners, Jean Francois Millet, 1857.

5

IN CHURCH AND MINISTRY

Ministry takes many forms. Ministry happens in everyday relationships with our families, friends, neighbors, and coworkers. It happens in spontaneous encounters with strangers. It happens in both planned and unplanned circumstances. Sometimes ministry is focused on a specific mission or target population. And, hopefully, ministry happens in our churches from week to week.

The essays in this chapter will flow from the heart outward. What are our motives in ministry, and how do we act with integrity as we minister to the saved and the unsaved? Next, we will explore relationships within the church. How do we honor and serve one another in the community of the local church? God's purposes in the church sometimes feel quite mysterious. But in the end, it all comes down to loving well and walking in the Spirit, which is where this chapter will land.

MOTIVES IN MINISTRY

Ministry in the kingdom of God can be tremendously fulfilling and joyful. We live to feel the Lord's smile upon us. We long to know that he is blessing our work with fruitfulness for his glory. It's one of the best feelings in the world.

But Christian ministry is also fraught with many hazards, as any experienced pastor or minister can tell you. Ministers who are not careful of their boundaries can very easily find themselves overworked, overwhelmed, or overcome by temptation and moral failure. Even those who are good at setting boundaries are not immune from intense pressure, hurt, and disappointment. This can lead to ethical compromise and impure motives.

Believers assume much about and demand much from their leaders, often unconsciously. There are unspoken expectations that in the kingdom of God, people—and leaders especially—should be more just, kind, honest, and fair than those who are overtly living by the world's standards. And this may be a reasonable assumption. But people are people everywhere, inside and outside the church. And where you have people, you have problems. The best of us are imperfect and are bound to disappoint others, despite our finest, most noble efforts.

Nevertheless, leaders are accountable to God for their leadership and for the ethics and motives that undergird it (Heb. 13:17). Much of Paul's second letter to the Corinthians is a defense of his leadership and a full disclosure of the motives of his heart. He argues fervently that his teaching and behavior toward them were the outworking of his inner motives. Because he worked so diligently to conform his heart to Christ's, this was to be the basis for their evaluation of his apostleship and provides a worthy standard for evaluating our own.

To drive home the point, Paul repeatedly contrasts right and wrong motives. He exhorts disciples of Christ to carefully discern what defines authentic, honorable ministry of the gospel. We must understand well what authentic, Christ-centered ministry looks like so we will recognize and avoid ministries driven by unholy motivations. I'll just give a summary and a few examples from Paul's very heartfelt letter.

Paul and his team of leaders were not operating from a hidden agenda, but from a burning desire to present the truth, commending it to "every man's conscience in the sight of God" (2 Cor. 4:2). He didn't ask the Corinthians for money, or praise, or recognition as someone great. He had brought his ego into submission with the word and will of God. He insists, "It is Christ's love that fuels our passion and motivates us" (5:14, TPT).

From there, we see that Paul stood in "holy awe of the Lord" (5:11, TPT). His fear of God prohibited him from ever handling the Word of God with trickery or deceptiveness. There were no confusing mixed messages. He didn't cover up or avoid confronting people with the truth, even when it stung.

In this letter, Paul expresses his anguish at having appeared harsh at times in his presentation of the truth. Yet he celebrates the fruit that resulted. In one of my favorite New Testament passages, Paul expresses great satisfaction with the Corinthians:

> Godly sorrow brings repentance that leads to salvation and leaves no regret, but worldly sorrow brings death. See what this godly sorrow has produced in you: what earnestness, what eagerness to clear yourselves, what indignation, what alarm, what longing, what concern, what readiness to see justice done. At every point you have proved yourselves. (7:10–11)

Paul demonstrates the heart that Jesus seeks in those who make disciples and lead them.

What is most compelling and convincing about the authenticity of Paul's ministry—one we should seek to emulate—is the high price he paid for the privilege. He presents "proof" of his legitimacy in chapter 6, detailing his endurance amid great hardships, stress, calamity, beatings, riots, hunger, and sleepless nights. Throughout every season, even when at death's door, he clung to truthful teaching, kindness, holiness, love, and full transparency.

This fearless apostle had a clear conscience, knowing that in his heart he had never betrayed the Lord or his people. Wouldn't we all like to be able to say the same thing at the end of our respective races? Whatever life and ministry throw at us, will we say truthfully in the end that our hearts were steadfast, true, and noble, motivated always by burning devotion to Jesus Christ, his Word, and his church? Let it be so, Lord.

WHY GO TO CHURCH?

It may strike you as self-evident that Christians are people who go to church. This is a common assumption. When I ask new clients about their faith or their spiritual journey, they will often respond with, "I go to church at…" Alternatively, they will say, "Well, I'm a spiritual person, but I don't go to church." Either way, I usually reply that I hadn't asked them about church. What I wanted to know was the nature of their relationship with God, not whether they show up at this or that building once a week.

This sometimes leads to a longer conversation about what church attendance means as an aspect of spirituality, and why people do or do not partake in corporate worship and fellowship. After many such conversations, I reflected more deeply on my own motivations to participate in worship services and other aspects of community life in a local church.

In my many years of fellowship with Jesus Christ and his followers, I may have missed weekly corporate worship about a dozen times. In these cases, I was sick, exhausted, traveling, or simply needing to be alone. But the next week, I've shown up to rejoin my spiritual tribe at church. There have been times when I was not happy with the church we were attending for a variety of reasons, but I went anyway. Why is this? Believe me, I know it is very easy to decide *not* to go.

The first reason—not the most spiritual or holy one—is that it is my habit. It is a healthy habit, like eating vegetables or taking my daily walks. It is part of the rhythm of my weeks and years and therefore helps to keep me grounded in all my other spiritual disciplines.

It is integral to my rule of life. I always go because I always go. I don't question it, like I don't question whether to brush my teeth in the morning.

I've questioned at times *where* I'm going to attend on a given Sunday, because I like to experience new worship environments from time to time. I've also been through many transitions in membership from one church to another. But I very rarely lack the motivation to go *someplace* where Christ-lovers are gathered to worship.

The second, the one that underlies all the rest, is that I love God. He says in his Book that he enjoys when people come together to worship and exalt him. So, I participate for his pleasure. I sing songs and dance and show him with my whole body and soul how much I appreciate his greatness and his goodness.

I bow publicly in confession, repentance, and awe, assured of his mercy and forgiveness toward all of us. I do these things at home alone as well, and always will. But extravagant praise and worship in community is in good times a feast and a celebration, and at difficult times a shared suffering in God's presence. Either way, I wouldn't forsake it for anything.

The third is that I love to hear the spoken Word of God, to bask in his truth as believers have done throughout the ages. Scripture is my treasured possession. I never take it for granted nor tire of hearing and studying it. I trust that God inspires messages in the hearts of his shepherds that will minister to those who come near to listen. My presence and attention demonstrate respect for God's Word and the men and women who are anointed and positioned to speak it into my life. I go to church to receive.

Related to this is the fourth reason I assemble with others. All that I receive through various spiritual practice, including corporate worship, should prepare and equip me to live in the light. Church on Sunday strengthens me to walk out the gospel from Monday to Saturday. I believe that what I receive from my participation in church must be put into practice. I'm reminded to be more present with people, more loving, more in tune with the wind of the Spirit blowing through my days (John 3:7–8).

Finally, I go because I am part of the body of Christ. Every part is needed, and when a part is missing, the body is not functioning in wholeness. I go because there may be someone there who needs what I bring. If I go with an open heart and an expectation to hear from the Holy Spirit, he will show me those who need a hug, a prayer, a Scripture, a word of encouragement. Maybe seeing my freedom in worship will give someone the courage to break free as well. These are the things I carry best, so I go to church to give them away.

I, in turn, need all that the other parts of the body have to give. I honor all the gifts I see around me, understanding that my walk with God is incomplete without the contribution of my beloved companions in the faith.

I'm grateful to live in a country where we can attend church without fear, and I pray America stays that way. But I'd like to believe that if I lived in China or Pakistan, or any other place where Christians are oppressed and persecuted, I would be among those who risk joining with others to praise and seek the face of God. The church is all of us, and we need one another.

BROTHERS AND SISTERS
OF OTHER MOTHERS

It seems like eons ago when I was preparing to be a professional jazz guitarist and vocalist. I was in college studying jazz. Jazz was the only music on my turntable. I practiced jazz tunes for hours every day. I sought out gigs of my own and live performances by some of the best musicians in the world. This was New York in the 1980s for me.

Sometimes my father would come into the city to hear me play or attend a jazz concert with me. He was always mystified by the non-verbal communication that takes place when a jazz band is improvising together. I would explain to him that the musicians are rooted in a common repertoire, moving through familiar harmonic structures, listening for a melody or rhythm to creatively add color and texture to the unique landscape of each song.

To this day, wherever I might travel, I could track down some jazz musicians, and we could play music together immediately even if we spoke different languages. The sound, the swing, the history and library of songs, and the adventure of improvisation would unite us. We're like brothers and sisters of other mothers, to borrow a phrase.

This phenomenon came to my mind while reading excerpts from Oswald Chambers' writings on prayer. I experienced some perplexity because of his lofty, old-school way of phrasing things. But then he quoted Scripture, and I felt instantly connected.

This can happen when exploring the theological works of any previous generation of "God chasers" throughout the history of the church. They all have unique styles of expression that reflect the era and distinct cultural environment in which they lived.

It may take effort to get to the core of their theology because of their context-specific idioms and cultural references. But it's worthwhile to take in what seems obscure at first, digest it, and contextualize it for our time and place. We can do this if we are convinced of the integrity of our same source: God's perfect Book.

The Scriptures are our common language and heritage. They transcend all time and space and cultural nuance. They connect you and me to the heart of Oswald's faith, or Martin Luther's, or Jonathan Edwards's, and that faith looks just like ours in the end.

Of course! They are brothers from other mothers, led and inspired by the wisdom of the same Father, reconciled by the same Jesus, led by the same Holy Spirit, instructed by the same words of wisdom.

You may have experienced this phenomenon when you've visited a church in an unfamiliar cultural environment. The worship style is different, and the service and fellowship have a different feel. But if brothers and sisters are preaching and worshipping in accordance with the truths of Scripture, there is a comfortable familiarity. Instead of distancing ourselves, we can come closer and enjoy their unique ways of loving God and each other.

As Bible-believing disciples of Christ, we have a family bond that goes much deeper than race, ethnicity, education level, social status, denomination, or any of the other descriptors that categorize and often divide us. Jesus is the "firstborn among many brothers and sisters" (Rom. 8:29), and we are those brothers and sisters!

God does not show partiality to individuals within his flock (Deut. 10:17; Acts 10:34), and we are not supposed to show partiality either (James 2:1–9; 1 Tim. 5:21). God's love compels us to walk in familial love for our brothers and sisters everywhere."

Like players in a jazz ensemble, we can jump into the creation of new sounds, colors, and rhythms, knowing that we are drawing from the same source. All of our unique contributions come together into a holy song that rises to the throne of God.

God rejoices in the united song of his people. And he rejoices when we understand and experience our family ties, recognizing that we are brothers and sisters of many mothers.

> How good and pleasant it is when God's people live together in unity! It is like precious oil poured on the head, running down on the beard, running down on Aaron's beard, down on the collar of his robe. It is as if the dew of Hermon were falling on Mount Zion. For there the Lord bestows his blessing, even life forevermore. (Ps. 133)

Jazz band in Paris, photo by Josephine Bevan.

THE UNLEAVENED BREAD OF SINCERITY AND TRUTH

Don't you know that a little yeast leavens the whole batch of dough? Get rid of the old yeast, so that you may be a new unleavened batch—as you really are. For Christ, our Passover lamb, has been sacrificed. Therefore, let us keep the Festival, not with the old bread leavened with malice and wickedness, but with the unleavened bread of sincerity and truth.

1 Cor. 5:6–8

The fifth chapter of Paul's first letter to the Corinthians tackles the ancient (*and* modern) issue of how the church is to address flagrant, unrepentant sin—sexual and otherwise—in a body of believers. The apostle Paul draws a clear distinction between two standards—one that applies to the family of God and another that applies to the pagan, unbelieving world. Followers of Jesus should not behave according to the spirit of the world or the age but allow the conviction of the Holy Spirit and the wisdom of the Word of God to direct them.

The metaphor Paul chose to illustrate this was leaven. This does not refer to yeast, but to a lump of fermented dough used to bake a batch of bread. Only a small amount is necessary to produce a large batch of puffy loaves of bread.

Paul rebuked church members for allowing a man to remain in

their fellowship after the disclosure that he'd been having incestuous relations with his father's wife. He warned that if they allowed this sin of one man to remain unaddressed, the sin would permeate the flock and defile the entire church. As a dedicated scholar of the Torah, Paul brought to their remembrance the unleavened bread of the Passover event, and the instruction given in the Law of Moses:

> Sacrifice as the Passover to the Lord your God an animal from your flock or herd at the place the Lord will choose as a dwelling for his Name. Do not eat it with bread made with yeast, but for seven days eat unleavened bread, the bread of affliction, because you left Egypt in haste—so that all the days of your life you may remember the time of your departure from Egypt." (Deut. 16:2-3)

The yearly sacrifice, accompanied by unleavened bread, was to be a very holy observance. It reminded them of the Lord's rescue from captivity. Passover reminded them that they were a people set apart from the world. It was a commemoration of their full dependence upon God for their very survival. It was a joyful but humbling feast, with nothing "puffed up" about it.

Leaven is a metaphor used frequently in Scripture. It usually refers negatively to the insidious, expanding qualities of sin, whether in an individual or in a body of believers. Jesus used the metaphor of leaven to refer to false doctrine, particularly the contorted and exploitive teachings of the religious leaders of his day. He warned his disciples to "take heed and beware against the leaven of the Pharisees and Sadducees" (Matt. 16:6).

The Pharisees were dangerous to the spreading of the gospel because of their oppressive legalism, and the Sadducees for their love of ecclesiastical prestige and wealth. Jesus did not want his followers puffed up with pride because of presumed religious correctness or perception of elite social status. He knew it would bloat and corrupt their characters. His was a gospel for sinners, for the poor in spirit, the meek, the mourners, those hungry and thirsty for righteousness.

Scripture exhorts us to be attentive to doctrine. Plain and unleavened. Right, biblical, Christ-centered, truth- and grace-centered doctrine matters. Good doctrine makes us wholesome and good, not puffy and prideful. Paul writes to the Corinthians,

> Therefore, let us keep the Festival, not with the old bread leavened with malice and wickedness, but with the unleavened bread of sincerity and truth. (1 Cor. 5:6–8)

I love a good piece of leavened, freshly baked bread. But this is figurative, of course. These Scriptures teach us not to *become* leavened. When we discern that we are under conviction over something that has crept into our hearts or our churches, however small or insignificant, we are to *purge it out.* If we do not, it might expand and take control, and spread to others whom we might negatively influence.

THE PUZZLE

I've always liked jigsaw puzzles. I enjoy the relaxing and invigorating mental exercise they provide. It is prudent to remember, before I take one out of the closet, that once I have started working one, I may feel compelled to finish it.

Even though I may be busy with other chores, every time I pass through the room where it lies, I will have to stop and find a piece or two. I must be willing to make a commitment of time, concentration, and space on the table for its completion.

Jigsaw puzzles remind me of the often-puzzling experiences of being a part of the body of Christ and of serving and worshipping in a local church. We come together, week after week, each bringing our own small and unique piece of the picture.

We are drawn back, again and again, by some strange determination and fragile hope that if we keep showing up, keep working hard, keep studying at it, keep concentrating…if we want it badly enough, the puzzle will one day soon start to look like something that makes sense. Even when frustrated, discouraged and weary, disappointed with our seeming lack of progress, we are drawn irresistibly back to the table. We want to see the thing finished.

Our worship to God seems, most of the time, piecemeal and scattered. The individual pieces have interesting colors and shapes, but in themselves they have no definition, no recognizable pattern. The random array of pieces seems to us to have no discernible order or beauty when compared with the vision of God we seek.

"Hear O ye people, the Lord is one" (Deut.6:4)—complete in himself, all One majestic whole, clothed in a seamless garment of holiness, exalted, perfect; we can only stand in this Presence with speechless awe.

Yet here we come, trying this piece here and that piece there. Prayer, intercession, preaching, teaching, serving, singing, dancing, bowing, lifting hands, tears, laughter, sacrifice, holy romance, surrender, sanctification, and on and on in our religious endeavors.

Once in a while we find a piece that fits and we shout, "Hallelujah!" (like a miner shouting "Eureka!" when striking gold after months of panning for it). We testify that for a moment, we have located God. We've come into contact; the pieces fit. God has heard and answered and has given us a moment of rest in him.

But the divine humor in this is that even when we experience fitting into the picture, we still can't see the picture. We are not high enough above it. And even if we were, we might be surprised to find that the picture is not coherent, because it isn't finished yet. Only God has the power to envision it done. He holds the box top.

God doesn't seem to be in a hurry to finish the puzzle he's designed. He wants us to keep coming back, making our feeble efforts toward a vision of him that our limited minds can comprehend. He enjoys our heartfelt songs, our fellowship, our acts of love and compassion. He is moved by them, in much the same way that we human parents are moved when watching our children perform in a pageant or school play. It is the very fact that the effort is so flawed, yet so sincere, that makes it so charming and endearing.

This puzzle we are working on is not an easy one. It is not the one we would have chosen from the shelf. The pieces are far too many and too small, the patterns far too complex, the level of difficulty deliberately beyond our aptitude on our own. There is mystery. We need help from the manufacturer.

We whine sometimes, "Can't you at least show us how it will turn out?" The only answer we receive is to look to the word pictures of one man who lived long ago, in a different time and culture. The only person who has ever been in God's picture and above the picture at the same time. The biblical portrait of a perfect man keeps drawing us back with his loving encouragement. "Abide in me," he says, "and I will abide in you" (John 15:4, KJC). "You will bear fruit, I promise. Our joy will be full!"

This piecing-together process of God's great puzzle seems to us so painstaking and long, requiring every bit of strength we can bring to it. We have to keep paying attention.

And once the picture is complete, what is to become of it?

Once my scene of some houses on a hill with horses and cows feeding on the grass and birds and clouds floating by is complete, what then? I may admire it for a little while, feeling some satisfaction, but before long it needs to be cleared away to make room for other things (like breakfast).

God—once his workmanship is complete, without spot, without blemish, without wrinkle—plans to sweep it up in himself! No longer itty-bitty pieces, but all of us made one with the perfect completeness of Almighty God.

In the end, there *is* satisfaction for all. For us—blessed relief. For the Holy Spirit (who has been whispering clues as we worked away)—the honor which is due him. For Jesus Christ—the privilege of putting in the glorious final piece; and for Father God—the joy of declaring, "Well done!"

AGING IN THE KINGDOM

Growing older, reaching an age considered "senior," can be quite disconcerting. Unless we die prematurely, we all face the challenges of old age. When that time arrives, what we could long deny through the magical, invincibility-fraught delusions of youth becomes inescapably real. Aches and pains, dyspepsia, insomnia, memory failures, etc.—these are symptoms not entirely unique to older individuals, but they are certainly more common as the body and mind lose some of their youthful elasticity and resiliency.

No one has an unconditional guarantee of long life. No one gets out of being a human being alive. Some age well, and some not so well.

Erik Erikson, a developmental theorist and contemporary of Sigmund Freud, believed that identity and personality continue to develop throughout all stages of life. He developed an elaborate, multistage theory of human development. The final developmental stage of his theory Erikson labeled "Integrity vs. Despair." This stage, which begins around age sixty, requires that we reflect on the past and make judgments about whether we have had a successful or meaningful life.

My interpretation of success in this stage is that we are able to say, in effect, "I may not have completed everything I wanted to do (yet), but my life has been productive and meaningful, and I have made a difference. Overall, I have lived a life of integrity." If we judge that our lives have been unproductive, guilt-ridden, or disappointing, we might experience despair and hopelessness. According to Erikson, successful navigation through this crisis will produce wisdom and the ability to accept death without fear. Visit any nursing home, and you will recognize individuals in both categories.

Erikson was a smart fellow, without a doubt. But what does the Bible teach us about growing old from God's perspective? A great deal, from beginning to end. In fact, there are blessings and advantages that come when a person of faith navigates these later years.

Older members of the family and community mentor and bless the next generations. Some examples are Moses and Joshua, Jacob with his sons, Eli with Samuel, David with Solomon, Paul with Timothy. As death approached the patriarchs, they solemnly spoke blessing and identity over their children. Moses commanded the Israelites to impart to their children all of the commandments of God, to "talk about them when you sit at home and when you walk along the road, when you lie down and when you get up" (Deut. 6:7). The aged Paul wrote to his protégé Timothy, "Do not neglect the gift, which was given you through a prophetic message when the body of elders laid their hands on you" (1 Tim. 4:14). Imagine how precious were these words to Timothy from his spiritual father!

Older saints encourage younger saints with their testimonies. The psalmist declared of God's faithfulness, "I was young and now am old, yet I have never seen the righteous forsaken or their children begging bread" (Ps. 37:25). Caleb, as he laid claim to his piece of the Promised Land, thanked and glorified God for giving him long life. He was still strong and vigorous at eighty-five years old, and received a special reward for his long, wholehearted obedience to the Lord (Josh. 14:6–14). Young soldiers must have been astonished and inspired by Caleb's courage and faithfulness. Paul claims that those who have "finished the race" and "kept the faith," will receive the crown of righteousness the Lord promises to the faithful (2 Tim. 4:7–8). It is older people who carry this perspective.

Older believers model steadfast faith. Abraham is the most prominent biblical example. This patriarch, already one hundred years old, with "his body as good as dead" (Rom. 4:19) never lost his faith in God's promise to bring him offspring. He was "fully persuaded that God had power to do what he had promised" (v. 21). Abraham's unwavering faith in God earned him the title of father to all who believe. Younger believers are without excuse for quitting or losing heart.

Spirit-filled elders intercede and prophesy to the church. The prophet Joel declared that when the Spirit came in fulness, "young and old, male and female, will dream dreams and prophecy" (Joel 2:28). Prophets Simeon and Anna, both quite aged physically and in the Lord, recognized the presence of the promised king and boldly prophesied over him when Mary and Joseph brought their child to the temple (Luke 2:25–38). Those with long experience in life are ideal mentors in the gifts of the spirit.

I could add more to this list, but I think I've made my point. Does the modern church at large take full advantage of the integrity and wisdom of her older members? It seems that many leaders, wanting to attract younger people, fail to mine the treasure that lies within their more seasoned brothers, sisters, fathers, and mothers. If we truly want to cultivate a culture of honor in the church, this is a good place to start.

COMMENDATION & CRITICISM

Paul's letter to the Romans remains one of the finest pieces of literature ever penned in any genre, loaded with spiritual insight, profound doctrinal truths, Jewish history, and sound instruction to the church at large. This letter lacks the rebukes found in Galatians or Colossians. Paul seemed very pleased with the church at Rome and longed to have the opportunity to visit them. It was not a church he had founded or established, so he was a bit more deferential in exercising his authority toward them.

Toward the end of his letter, Paul praises the Roman believers with this affirming statement: "I myself am convinced, my brothers, you yourselves are full of goodness, complete in knowledge, and competent to instruct one another" (Rom. 15:14). This is just one of his general votes of confidence in the church at Rome. Paul shows excellent leadership skill by commending faithful followers in this way. He solicits their prayers for him, considering them worthy peers and partners in ministry. According to Paul, they had embraced the heart of the gospel message and had begun in large numbers to live what Tim Keller calls a "gospel-shaped life."

Paul then names *twenty-eight* individuals who had impacted his ministry and the advancement of the kingdom of God. He commends them for these things, among others: being among the first to model Christian faith; risking their lives or going to prison for the sake of the gospel; faithfully leading their house churches; helping those in need; working hard for the benefit of others; mothering him when he needed a mother; being worthy of honor; being truly good men and women, whom "the Lord picked out to be his very own" (16:1-13, NLT).

It is heartwarming to see this individual, public recognition for those who had served unselfishly in Christ. Exhortation is an essential motivational gift in the body of Christ. Paul models this in his letter, expressing words of affirmation, encouragement, and thanks to whom it is due.

There is something else that Paul teaches at the close of his letter. He warns the Roman church about those who are not walking admirably or honorably. He writes, "Watch out for people who cause divisions and upset people's faith by teaching things contrary to what you have been taught. Stay away from them. Such people are not serving Christ our Lord; they are serving their own personal interests. By smooth talk and glowing words, they deceive innocent people" (16:17–18, NLT). Notice that Paul doesn't call out these people by name, as he does in his pastoral epistles. He simply describes the indicators that an individual is not accurately representing Christ and warns the believers not to become yoked with them.

It is hurtful in the church when ministers publicly condemn or criticize other ministers by name without sufficient evidence that the ministers in question are causing division, teaching false doctrine, or seeking to deceive. This is still happening today. Often it is demoralizing to the church and a very bad witness to the secular world that is watching how we respond to conflict. We must be quick to commend those who are serving well, and very slow to criticize those with whom we might disagree, especially when our disagreement is based on strictly religious, tribal preferences.

We ought to be quick to honor and commend others for their kingdom work, or their perseverance, or their character, or their abounding love for others. We ought to seek them out and tell them how much we appreciate them. And we ought to be slow to speak badly about other leaders unless we truly believe they are bringing harm to the church. Even then we should do it with great caution, and in consultation with other leaders.

It's important that we master commending others as an aspect of the kingdom of heaven, that we might receive the commendation of heaven!

HOW TO
APPROACH A KING

I know I am not alone in my fascination with the series *The Crown*. It follows the British monarchy from the era of Edward VIII's abdication of the throne, the reign until death of his brother George VI, and the ongoing reign of Queen Elizabeth II. The royals still enjoy popularity around the world today.

Some observers attribute this to a universal desire among we commoners to feel part of a grand historical tradition, one full of drama, wealth, romance, and adventure. We want to connect with something that is nothing like our ordinariness.

Others strongly object to the whole idea of royalty, finding such institutionalized elitism politically incorrect in the extreme. Either way, fascination with royalty persists.

As someone who habitually relates everything to Scripture, I'm interested in how kings and queens are treated in Bible narratives. There is a protocol for being in the presence of royalty, and there are consequences for disrespecting the rules of approach. Throughout the Old Testament, and especially with the Davidic dynasty, approaching a king incorrectly could bring a death sentence. We see scores of characters in the chronicles of the kings of Israel and Judah who fell on their faces to give homage to even the most wretched of kings.

One of my favorite examples is Abigail, who so impressed David with her respectful approach that he married her (see 1 Samuel 25)! Even in the pagan world, kings and queens were to receive extraordinary honor and deference by all. We see this in Esther's fear of approaching her own husband, the king, without his summoning her. By Persian law, this could have condemned her to death.

In his weekly audience with Queen Elizabeth, Winston Churchill (played stunningly by John Lithgow in *The Crown*) portrays this attitude toward royals. Though three times her age, with a lifetime of heroic leadership on the world stage behind him, his demeanor becomes imbued with awe and quiet reverence when he enters the drawing room of the queen. He demurely kisses her hand. When departing, he backs out of the room to avoid turning his back to her. These are only a couple of the "rules" for showing respect for a king or queen, even in our postmodern era.

In a democratic republic, we Americans don't have this knowledge of protocol embedded in our DNA or collective history. We are, above all things, egalitarian in our contemporary ethics. This is not a terrible thing in itself. But there is a potential downside to this: We have a difficult time showing honor where honor is due. In government, in business, and even in the church.

Danny Silk, in his book *Culture of Honor*, emphasizes the importance of acknowledging who individuals are and the spiritual gifts they bring to the body, and honoring them in their uniqueness. This works in our vertical relationship with God and in our horizontal relationships with the family of God.

In the church, the lyrics to many of our praise and worship songs portray Jesus Christ as our everlasting, majestic King of all kings. We invite him near, that we might experience his presence among us. And we often do sense his glory in our midst.

I'm not trying to step on anyone's toes here, but—do we act in our worship gatherings as if we really believe we are in the presence of a king? Do we respect this king as we would respect an earthly king or queen, or even a president or prime minister? We are on level ground with one another, but he is exalted high above all creation. The fact that he has granted us intimate access to him doesn't mean we should approach him casually or thoughtlessly. He has raised his scepter to us. How, then, are we to approach him?

A short answer is that we are to seek his pleasure and not our own. I'm not suggesting rigid formalism or religiosity. Jeans and T-shirts are great as long as the hearts of the people wearing them carry a sincere reverence for the King. Spontaneous expressions of praise and worship are wonderful as long as they point toward the One to whom all honor is due.

When he is manifestly present with us, we are truly standing on holy ground. That's not a time to be rude, sloppy, or insincere in our devotion, but an opportunity to behold the glory of the King.

6

IN PSYCHOLOGY AND THERAPY, PART 1: PRINCIPLES

*Who has known the mind of the Lord so as to
instruct him? But we have the mind of Christ.*

1 Corinthians 2:16

Being a disciple of Jesus Christ in this beautiful, strange, and twisted world is challenging at best. As the apostle Paul noted, when one becomes a born-again believer, the struggle against the sin nature is starkly revealed. Blessedly, the Holy Spirit assists the believer in the process of becoming more Christlike. But because we continue to navigate in cultures that are antagonistic to our faith, we need to attain a perspective on who we are, whose we are, and where we stand in the battle.

I believe that studying psychology as well as normal and abnormal patterns of human development contributes to this perspective. As a student and then a professor of psychology, I amassed a wealth of examples. Wherever psychology agrees with Scripture, we can use it to our benefit; and wherever it disagrees, it is to be challenged or rejected.

The writings in the next two chapters are reflections on some of the psychological processes that can be connected meaningfully to our journey of faith. Part 1 focuses on some principles and theories in psychology, and Part 2 provides some stories of ways I've put principles into practice as a therapist. I offer them to provoke thought about the possibilities and limitations of human consciousness, as guided by the Holy Spirit, and to promote healing, cleansing, and growth.

ACCOMMODATING
FOR THE REVELATION
OF THE CHRIST

Gospel accounts of the ministry of Jesus often reveal how spiritually immature and emotionally unstable his disciples were. They were chaotic in their reactions to what they saw Jesus doing and to what they heard him teaching. They exhibited on various occasions the behavioral manifestations of jealousy and competitiveness, terror and confusion, ignorance and doubt, anger and hardness of heart.

I can point this out and still respect and honor them for their part in the gospel story. They couldn't help these reactions to Jesus any more than we could if we had been in their shoes. They could only know what they could know at the time. They were still captive to their carnal understanding. They had not yet been filled with the Spirit. They weren't from the scholarly rabbinical class that had a scriptural explanation handy for the phenomena they were witnessing.

But the most important thing to remember is that they were witnessing someone and something that had never existed before—the Christ. The disciples couldn't just assimilate him into a pre-existing conceptual model. He didn't meet their religious or political expectations. How could they fully comprehend the presence of a humble, gentle servant leader who was also a miracle-making superhero? How could they make sense of his proclamations that he, the only begotten Son of God, would be nailed on a cross, dead for three days, and raised again?

Assimilation, in the context of psychology, is an important aspect of learning, as observed and theorized by Swiss psychologist Jean Piaget. Imagine a child learning the concept of *bird* by observing a robin and then hearing Mom say, "See the birdie?" The child begins to construct a mental category ("birds") and can then assimilate other creatures into that category that resemble the prototype. Hummingbirds, eagles, ostriches, and chickens—all very different from each other in size and appearance—can still be readily understood to be in the category of birds, even by a young child. All these species of birds meet the criteria to identified as such (i.e., they have beaks and wings, lay eggs, etc.).

There is a second learning process called accommodation. This is when, for example, the child who has internalized the concept of *bird* sees a fish for the first time. His brain looks for a model in which to fit this new experience and finds none. He can tell it doesn't match *bird*. He must accommodate by creating a new category called *fish*. Once he does this, goldfish, catfish, and sharks have a place to fit into his understanding of the world.

Within the sociocultural environment of first-century Israel, the disciples knew how to identify a rabbi, a priest, a tax collector, a shepherd, a fisherman, or a soldier. They were aware of the more subtle distinctions between say, Jews and Samaritans. These were existing categories that allowed them to identify and assimilate people into their social context.

Then along came Jesus, down from heaven, with words and works never heard or seen before. Son of God and Son of Man, Messiah, Healer, Redeemer. He was the Word made flesh, firstborn from the dead, full of grace and truth. He was a creative Spirit, then a baby conceived in the womb of a Jewish girl. Then he grew to be a perfectly godly man, then a powerful teacher and prophet, full of the Holy Spirit. Then he became a suffering servant who endured a criminal's punishment. Then a resurrected king, the firstborn from the dead.

Jesus's disciples—including us—at some point must make this

accommodation; he cannot be assimilated into a pre-existing category. We must make room for him in our consciousness. We must come to understand that this one person defies all categories and conceptual models. He is our prototype of the perfect man, our only completely satisfactory example of what we'd like to be.

THE ASSUMPTION
OF GOOD WILL

Sometimes the people in our lives behave in confusing or offensive ways. Sometimes we don't even understand or approve of our own behavior. Over the lifespan, each of us develops explanatory models to assist us in understanding our own and others' behavior. Unfortunately, these models can be highly subject to error.

One of the most common errors is what social psychologists label *fundamental attribution error.* This means that when people behave in ways we don't like—cut us off in traffic or cut in line at the market, for example—we tend to assume that they have some sort of internal character defect of laziness, carelessness, or selfishness. In contrast, when we go to explain our own similar behavior, we attribute it to external forces and circumstances.

In other words, when I am the one in the wrong, I claim to have a good excuse or justification based on my circumstances. I assert that I'm a very good person in spite of my momentary rudeness or carelessness. But when you are in the wrong, it must be that there is something fundamentally wrong with you!

I've discovered that the assumption of good will is a great way to counteract this error. It works like this. Key relationships require a level of trust if they are to be healthy. I must be able to assume you have good will toward me, as I direct my good will toward you. This means that you can trust that as much as it lies in me, I will always seek what is good for you. I genuinely want life to go well for you, and I'm not just in it for myself. And my assumption is that you hold the same intention toward me.

Because it is based in subjective assumptions, and no one is perfect, there is an element of vulnerability in the assumption of good will. For instance, before I see a new counseling client for the first time, I assume that he or she will bring goodwill into the new relationship. In other words, my client, who is seeking help from me, is not going to try to hurt me in the process. This keeps me open, friendly, kind, and curious as I begin to get to know him or her.

I could be proven wrong and have been on rare occasions. But I maintain the practice of the assumption of good will because most of the time I do experience good will. Could it be that the expectation of good will directly influences the outcome, like a self-fulfilling prophecy? Could it also be true that despite the sin, evil, and brokenness of the world around us, there are more basically good-willed citizens than bad-willed ones? I'll leave that question for observers more astute than I.

I believe that assuming good will is an essential element of honor within spiritual communities. It is pleasing to the Lord when we forgo our paranoia and skepticism and expect from others a good and godly response when we extend ourselves toward them.

When Jesus sent out his disciples, he prepared them with the expectation that they would come across individuals of good will who would bless their mission and show them hospitality. The Bible does not record any of the names of these willing souls they encountered on their journey. But it does say that the disciples returned with glowing reports of widespread healing and deliverance as the demons fled from them. They must have found persons of good will who gave them places to stay and offered other forms of assistance while they fulfilled their mission. They may have had to shake off some "dust" of bad will off their feet as well, but if so, it did not prevent their overall success.

Jesus and his apostles who gave us the Scriptures consistently teach us to love our enemies, with the result that they become no longer enemies. If we insist on seeing them as enemies, we will be unable to bring the gospel of the kingdom to them. We will be defensive and unable to walk in good will. But if we suspend our assumption of enemy status, we are allowing the possibility that our influence will warm them, feed them, and change their hearts toward God.

It is natural and understandable that those who have been hurt a lot by people they trusted will struggle more with the assumption of good will. But if we are to follow closely in the steps of the Master, we must imitate his openness, vulnerability, and compassion toward those who came into his presence.

LISTENING AS
AN ACT OF LOVE

As an educator and supervisor of counselors newly entering the field, one of my responsibilities is to coach them in the art of listening. I consider this the most important intervention in therapy when helping individuals and couples heal fractured relationships—to train them to truly listen to others in a constructive and loving way. So, it stands to reason that the counselor should be able to practice and model excellent listening skills.

Many lay people I talk to feel that they are good listeners. I suppose they assume this because friends or family members seek them out to talk to them about their problems. Indeed, some individuals are more naturally gifted than others with the capacity to listen well. But in my experience great listeners are pretty rare.

Listening is actually very hard work; and most of us, without intentional effort and even a bit of training, don't do it very well. Think about it: it is one of the main reasons counselors are required to go to counselor school and complete long internships before they are unleashed upon the public. Anyone can learn to speak well by speaking a lot. But we often take listening for granted and assume that we've got it covered without working on it. This complacency about listening causes an incredible amount of pain in relationships.

M. Scott Peck, in his well-known book *The Road Less Traveled: A New Psychology of Love, Traditional Values and Spiritual Growth*, offers a compelling analysis of the relationship between listening and loving. He starts with the concept that love, to truly be love, requires either work, or courage, or both. When we extend ourselves to others, we must overcome inertia to move into a work of love or press through fear with courage when love involves risk and vulnerability. Peck further explains that the primary work in loving others is giving them the gift of our full attention, and listening is the primary form of giving our attention.

How we all need to be listened to! I've often said that if people could learn to listen to one another, I'd be out of business…and that would be just fine with me. Everyone would feel so loved that I'd quit being a counselor and open a flower shop or something fun like that.

We instinctively know when someone has really heard us, and there are few things in life that are more healing and validating. David Augsburger has said, "Being heard is so close to being loved that for the average person, they are almost indistinguishable."[1]

I witness this in marital therapy all the time. Slowing down the communication process so that each speaker knows he or she has really been heard fundamentally transforms the atmosphere of the relationship. It invites intimacy and emotional safety. It demonstrates love in the most powerful way I know.

Jesus was a wonderful listener. He listened perfectly to his Father, always acting in accordance with the Father's word and will. He also listened to people with wholehearted interest when their motives were sincere and rooted in faith. Based on their questions and concerns, he offered responses that, even when provocative or challenging, promoted life and hope. Notable examples are the Samaritan woman of John 4, Nicodemus in John 3, and his ongoing dialogues with his closest disciples in John 13–16.

The Bible, and especially the Wisdom Literature, exhorts us to listen to God, and to listen to the wise counsel of others. This is key to living a fruitful life. The apostle James commanded by the Holy Spirit that "everyone should be quick to listen, slow to speak and slow

---

1. David Augsburger, *Caring Enough to Hear and Be Heard: How to Hear and How to Be Heard in Equal Communication.* Ventura, CA: Regal Books, an imprint of Gospel Light, 1982.

to become angry" (James 1:19). I'm reminded of the quip about having two ears and only one mouth, indicating that we should listen at least twice as much as we speak.

If we desire to become better listeners, a good place to start is to notice what happens mentally when our conversation partner is speaking, and it is our turn to listen. We might be graciously giving eye contact and nodding our head to indicate attention, while actually we're thinking about what we are going to say as soon as there is a pause (or maybe thinking about what we're going to cook for dinner). If we had to accurately paraphrase what the person said, we might be at a loss.

If we catch ourselves doing this, we can intentionally practice the discipline of putting our own thoughts to the side and listening with the goal of being able to reflect and validate what the person has said. Carl Rogers called this *accurate empathy*. It is at the heart of most healing and change.

This type of listening calls for delayed gratification, which is an essential aspect of maturity. Patience, grasshopper; you'll get your turn. In fact, if your friend, spouse, client, or child really feels heard—and therefore loved—by you, they are going to be much more likely to want to hear what you have to say when it's your turn.

God, help us to listen with loving ears and our whole hearts, and thereby love one another well.

BLAMELESSNESS AND MORAL DEVELOPMENT

The Psalms comprise a portion of the Hebrew worship songbook, and they cover a wide array of subjects. They are full of prayer, praise, worship, and theological truths. They also uncover matters of the heart, relationships, and the drama of being human.

Some of the earlier psalms focus on justice versus injustice, integrity versus deceit, moral depravity versus purity and blamelessness. These are among the many instances in which the Scriptures draw a contrast between good and evil, in their many forms. In one example David, the sweet psalmist of Israel, declares before the Lord,

> Though you probe my heart,
> though you examine me at night and test me,
> you will find that I have planned no evil;
> my mouth has not transgressed.
> Though people tried to bribe me,
> I have kept myself from the ways of the violent
> through what your lips have commanded.
> My steps have held to your paths;
> my feet have not stumbled. (Ps. 17:3–5)

These declarations bring to mind a detailed theory of moral development advanced by a psychologist named Lawrence Kohlberg.

Kohlberg's theory is rooted in a study in which he told stories to subjects of various ages about people facing difficult moral dilemmas, and then asked them a series of questions to ascertain their moral decision-making processes. Kohlberg theorized that like physical, cognitive, sexual, and psychosocial growth in individuals, moral development occurs gradually, in a series of discernible stages.

According to this theory, the most primitive state is the *preconventional* stage, in which the locus of moral decision-making is fear of punishment. Young children or underdeveloped adults may choose to do right only if they fear the consequences. They don't want to risk the pain and humiliation of punishment because of their actions, so they make choices they believe will keep them out of trouble.

The middle stages, which Kohlberg calls *conventional,* are rooted in conformity to social norms. People at this level choose to follow the rules because of a fear of rejection or expulsion from their social group. They depend upon conformity with social norms for their sense of security. Moral choices are based on preserving the approval of others. Think of the parents of the blind man in John 9. They would not glorify God for their son's healing because they feared excommunication from the synagogue for recognizing Jesus as the Healer.

At the top of the scale of moral development, which Kohlberg labeled "postconventional," is the determination to respond to the inner voice of conscience, placing concern for others over concern for self. Individuals with a highly developed moral compass do what they believe is right based on *eternal* and *internal* principles. Their moral integrity comes from the inside—from the heart, where the Bible locates the source of either our holiness or our defilement. At this level, individuals insist on maintaining a pattern of righteousness regardless of punishment, rejection, persecution, or death. This is the level of Jesus and the apostles.

This is the level of blamelessness, and there are very few who fully achieve it. But as Christ-followers, he has set us free from sin so that we are enabled to pursue holiness, to become "blameless and pure, children of God, without fault in a crooked and depraved nation, in which [we] shine like starts in the universe…" (Phil. 2:15).

If we achieve this level, we don't lie, but not because we're afraid of punishment or shame. No, we don't lie because we're not liars. We don't steal because we're not thieves. We don't kill because we're not murderers. Evil is not in there, so it doesn't work itself out.

At this level that Jesus makes possible through his redemptive life within, we can fearlessly live in love, grace, and peace, no matter how others choose to treat us. Oswald Chambers wrote, "From the Lord's standpoint it does not matter whether I am defrauded or not; what does matter is that I do not defraud."[1]

We can be blameless, causing no harm to others or to the testimony of the goodness and holiness of God. Does this seem like too great an expectation of ourselves? I don't think so, or God wouldn't require it. He wants us pure, clean, and blameless, the spotless bride he will one day give as a gift to his Son.

---

1. Oswald Chambers, *My Utmost for His Highest.* Ulrichsville, OH: Barbour and Company, 1963.

ZOOMING IN AND ZOOMING OUT

It's been my experience and observation that often life's problems come in bunches. We encounter "trials of many kinds" (James 1:2) while trying to keep up with the normal stresses and irritations of daily life. Marital conflict, parenting dilemmas, financial pressures, job loss, disease, accidents, sick or dying loved ones, etc.—these can pile up to test or even threaten our faith.

We might obsessively focus on one issue and neglect others that are equally important or more important. Or we might be afraid to focus on potential solutions to one problem because we feel overwhelmed by the whole array of them. Either way, we are apt to get stuck or begin to despair.

In his teaching, Jesus often focused his audience's imagination on small, natural things like seeds, flowers, birds, coins, trees, sheep, goats, or fish. He did this to help them understand metaphorically the vast realities of salvation, discipleship, or the love of God. At other times, he challenged them to comprehend those grand realities directly, by citing Old Testament prophets or praying to the Father while they listened in. He taught his disciples about the kingdom of heaven, helping them recognize that it was all around them in the infinite beauty and detail of God's creation. He had a great ability to zoom in and zoom out.

This concept underlies the language of the gestalt, developed as a psychological theory in the 1930s, and subsequently applied in therapeutic interventions. It recognizes that individuals can perceive pictures and problems in their details, or as a whole, or in both ways. Ideally, we can shift our consciousness to take both aspects of experience into consideration.

As a counselor, over the years I've encountered people who become obsessed with the concrete details of an issue and lose all perspective on the big picture. They cannot comprehend the underlying meaning in their distress or conflict. I've also encountered many who are living in a cloud of worry over the enormity of a problem and can't recognize small details or actions that might actually help to resolve a problem. Both indicate a fixed-lens approach, when what they need is a spiritual lens that can zoom in to clearly see the smallest details and can zoom out to see the whole scene panoramically.

God promises to give us the wisdom we need; we just need to ask him (James 1:5). But I've found that we often also need a friend or a counselor to help us adjust our lenses and become more flexible in our point of view. We need each other at times when we can't chase away obsessive thoughts on our own. And we also need each other when we can't seem to focus on an issue long enough to see a solution, a path forward, or even a way of coping.

God helps us to zoom in and zoom out, and our brothers and sisters in Christ can help us too. It's wise to access all available sources of godly understanding and perspective. We need to remain in his light (1 John 1:7); as we do this over time, our spiritual lenses become more adaptive and responsive. We become able to clearly see both the step we are on and the distant horizon.

PRESSURE AND PAIN

You may be familiar with comic Brian Regan's very funny sketch about pressure and pain. He observes that doctors don't like to use the word "pain":

"Doctors will tell you about 'pressure.' If a doctor tells you you're about to feel some pressure, buckle up…. He could be swinging a two-by-four at your head: 'In a moment you're going to feel a little bit of pressure.'" His sarcastic reply: "Hey, bring it on—I'm good under pressure!"[1]

But seriously, there is a difference. It's a difference that was illustrated in living color when I was the clinical director of a program for young women who had been trafficked or otherwise exploited. One of the best therapeutic tools we had to offer them was equine-assisted learning, with the assistance of our two white horses, Ranger and Minnie.

At one point the facilitator spoke about how the two concepts of pressure and pain register to the psyche of horses. She shared that for a horse, pressure comes from being pestered, distracted, or provoked by a person or animal smaller than he. The most likely response to this nonlethal threat is for the horse to turn away from the pressure and walk away. If he can't get away, he may wait nervously for the annoyance to go away. Pull back his ears, make some noise, swish his tail.

Pain is different. Pain for a horse comes from threatening motions by a predator who can kill him—a grizzly, a mountain lion, or a pack

---

1. Brian Regan comedy sketch accessed at https://www.youtube.com/watch?v=zfy_-F4Yaa8.

of wolves. After millennia of surviving and adapting to many environmental threats, horses have learned the distinction between pressure and pain, using it to determine when to run away and when to move toward the source of potential pain and overpower it.

The apostle James discusses this theme in his letter. Here it is in the Message:

> Consider it a sheer gift, friends, when tests and challenges come at you from all sides. You know that under *pressure*, your faith-life is forced into the open and shows its true colors. So don't try to get out of anything prematurely. Let it do its work, so you become mature and well-developed, not deficient in any way. (James 1:2–4, emphasis added)

Later in the same chapter, he continues:

> Don't let anyone under *pressure* to give in to evil say, "God is trying to trip me up." God is impervious to evil and puts evil in no one's way. The temptation to give in to evil comes from us and only us. We have no one to blame but the leering, seducing flare-up of our own lust. Lust gets pregnant and has a baby: sin! Sin grows up to adulthood and becomes a real killer. (James 1:13–15, emphasis added)

According to James, writing by inspiration of the Spirit, pressure in the form of trials and temptations is guaranteed to come—but we have been given the grace and power to withstand it.

Paul commends the believers in the churches of Macedonia whose response to one kind of pressure—financial—was to become more generous (2 Cor. 8:1–4). They were like grapes that, when crushed, gave forth the best, most fragrant juice. The psalmist observes, "As pressure and stress bear down on me, I find joy in your commands" (Ps. 119:142–144 NLT).

For us, taunts and temptations create pressure that requires us to take care, take cover, or take flight in a direction other than whence they came.

But pain is different, our horse lady continued to explain. Pain makes us rise up and confront it. We have to approach it, acknowledge its reality, and find a way through it. If we ignore or run away from this symptom, it may pursue us, find us, and eat us alive.

When we face pain head on, we may find a huge blessing on the other side. Jesus taught,

> "When a woman gives birth, she has a hard time, there's no getting around it. But when the baby is born, there is joy in the birth. This new life in the world wipes out memory of the *pain*. The sadness you have right now is similar to that *pain*, but the coming joy is also similar. When I see you again, you'll be full of joy, and it will be a joy no one can rob from you. You'll no longer be so full of questions." (John 16:21–23 MSG, emphasis added)

This is the pain of labor, the perseverance of hope, the discipline of faith. All of these things we must endure in the waiting.

Sometimes the pain is of our own making, and so is its cure. Paul praised the Corinthians for the fact that after he had called out a corporate sin that brought shame, they went headlong into a pain called "godly sorrow" that produced the fruits of repentance and turned them back to God. He observed that they had become "more alive, more concerned, more sensitive, more reverent, more human, more passionate, more responsible." (2 Cor. 7:11 MSG) The pain had truly changed them from the inside out. How beautiful that in God, the things that are most painful are the things that are most fruitful afterward.

Finally, the Bible warns us of the dangers of *not* allowing ourselves to feel pain. Avoidance distorts our thinking and deadens us to the voice of God. I've often observed that people who put a lot of energy into avoiding pain get to the point where they can't feel anything. Paul speaks of people who feel no pain over their own sinful behavior and "let themselves go in sexual obsession, addicted to every sort of perversion" (Eph. 4:19 MSG). Those are harsh words, but true.

Jesus set the example in this as in all good things:

During the days of Jesus' life on earth, he offered up prayers and petitions with loud cries and tears to the one who could save him from death, and he was heard because of his reverent submission…he learned obedience from what he suffered…(Heb. 5:7-8).

Peter sums it up well: "Since Christ suffered physical pain, you must arm yourselves with the same attitude he had, and be ready to suffer, too" (1 Peter 4:1, NLT).

I'm thankful to have learned from our equine facilitators how to move away from pressures that merely distract and torment, and toward the pains that propel us to growth and glory. This is how we imitate our Lord.

Three Graceful Horses, photo by Fabian Burkhardt, 2016.

SOBRIETY

Sobriety is a word so beautiful when spoken by recovering alcoholics or addicts celebrating freedom from controlling addictions. My big brother is one of them. He calls me now and then and reports to me, "I'm still sober," and I give joyful thanks and praise to God every time.

If you ask those who have gotten sober, they will tell you that there is a lot more to it than merely abstaining from a particular mind-altering substance or behavior. Sobriety encompasses a comprehensive life change—in thinking, behavior, emotional regulation, relationship, purpose, and value system.

The founders of the Twelve Steps of Alcoholics Anonymous understood this well. Though AA has been adapted to be applicable to a diversity of worldviews, its founders were Christians, and the Steps started and ended with God, their "higher power."

The program starts with confessing helplessness to manage our own lives and surrendering our unmanageable lives to God. We ask him to restore us to sanity. We accept conviction over our harmful behavior, seek to make amends, and commit to following a more honest, morally clean life. The pièce de résistance is Step 12:

> Having had a spiritual awakening as the result of these Steps, we tried to carry this message to alcoholics, and to practice these principles in all our affairs.

Sobriety turns out to be a spiritual awakening, with a message to share with others who long to be awakened. It sounds a lot like repentance to me, and receiving one of the fruits of repentance, a sober mind. A sober mind allows us to live a principled, righteous life. A sober mind gives us a capacity to overcome self-obsession and begin serving others.

Did you know that the Bible speaks in many places about the need to be sober, or sober-minded? It is one of the benefits of the new birth, as well as a characteristic of a maturing disciple. One of the most familiar passages is this:

> Be sober, be vigilant; because your adversary the devil walks about like a roaring lion, seeking whom he may devour. (1 Pet. 5:8, NKJV)

Sobriety means we aren't asleep at the switch, or under the influence of any worldly power. If we are to avoid the plans the enemy has for us, we must be sober and watchful.

The same writer, Peter, also tells us that when our minds are "alert and fully sober," they become more hopeful also, joyfully watching for the return of Jesus Christ. We receive power not to conform to our former desires, but to live in obedience to God, continual prayer, and a love for others that "covers a multitude of sins" (1 Pet. 1:13–14; 4:7–8). Don't we want to grab onto that way of living and not let go?

The apostle Paul, after exhorting disciples to become living sacrifices as their "reasonable service," admonishes them:

> Do not think of yourself more highly than you ought, but rather think of yourself with sober *judgment, in accordance with the faith God has distributed to each of you.* (Rom. 12:3, emphasis added)

This expresses another important aspect of having a sober, sound mind—that we have a realistic, honest appraisal of our own strengths and weaknesses. In my encounters with recovering addicts, this is one of the most refreshing aspects of their awakening. They are able to admit their faults, and at the same time, discover the ways that God has gifted them with strengths and talents. They—and all of us—need to understand how God wants to use us, even in our weaknesses, as he has uniquely fashioned us.

Some passages in the New Testament are more literal in their use of the two Greek words translated "sober." In the Pastoral Epistles to Timothy and Titus, sobriety is a way of life expected of elders, deacons, older men, older women, young men, and young women. No one is left out of the call to be moderate in their the use of alcohol.

But, this doesn't *just* mean that we don't become drunk and disorderly. Other words used in connection to this picture of sobriety are *discipline, dignity, self-control, faith, love, patient endurance, purity, devotion, hospitality, nobility, integrity,* and *wholesomeness* (Titus 2:1–7). As I said, comprehensive life transformation comes with a sound mind. It's a whole package.

There is a sense in which every compulsive, sinful behavior can be characterized as lust—an inordinate, illicit craving for something to satisfy our fleshly desires. When we begin to live our lives in God, the flesh still lusts against the Spirit. But the good news is that the Spirit fights back. If we commit our time, energy, attention, and will into the keeping of the Holy Spirit, he will help us. He will show us the way to keeping our hearts and minds pure.

I'll finish with Paul's wonderful exhortation to the Thessalonians. It applies to all who put their trust in the Lord Jesus Christ, and want to please him in every way:

> You are all children of the light and children of the day. We do not belong to the night or to the darkness. So then, let us not be like others, who are asleep, but let us be awake and sober. For those who sleep, sleep at night, and those who get drunk, get drunk at night. But since we belong to the day, let us be sober, putting on faith and love as a breastplate, and the hope of salvation as a helmet. (1 Thess. 5:5–8)

We don't need alcohol, drugs, or any other life-controlling compulsion if we can embrace this joyful path of sobriety in the Lord.

IN PSYCHOLOGY AND THERAPY, PART 2: PRACTICE

DANGER AND OPPORTUNITY

In Chinese, the character for the concept of "crisis" is a combination of "danger" and "opportunity." There is a danger to physical or psychological safety, and an opportunity to respond. A crisis requires some sort of response.

All around the world, people are experiencing major crises these days. Earthquakes and tsunamis, hurricanes and homelessness, famines and genocides, overdoses and suicides, terrorism and mass shootings, plagues and rampant social unrest. These events are danger and opportunity on the grandest scale.

Beyond the danger of the events themselves, we understand the long-term damage these traumatic experiences inflict on fragile human bodies and souls. But we also see the opportunity for people to come together in new ways to help each other to recover stability. The result often is a stronger sense of community, heroism, and charity.

On a smaller scale, in my general counseling practice, I see both danger and opportunity in most of the problems clients bring to me—sudden losses, too much change at once, relationship dysfunction, chronic illnesses, and numerous other threats to mental health. The danger is ongoing mental confusion, chaos, or complete loss of hope. The opportunity is to learn new ways of understanding and responding to difficulties and to draw nearer to God.

With couples who have neglected their relationship, often one or the other partner will consciously or unconsciously create a crisis that forces them into therapy. Often it is an extramarital affair, but it also might be an alcohol binge that ends in a DUI, or a secret, devastating financial decision. Whatever the crisis, they typically see it as a danger to the marital bond, and I agree.

But it is also an opportunity. The opportunity is to open a previously closed-off, dying family system to outside intervention and set the couple on a path toward healing and transformation. If they will face the process wisely, they often arrive at a much more satisfying relationship than what existed before the onset of the crisis.

Crises have this potential to teach and transform. We typically experience them as painful disruptions in the normal course of events. We must find some means of coping with and adapting to reality.

We instinctively try to resist pain. But as C. S. Lewis so wisely wrote, "We can ignore even pleasure. But pain insists upon being attended to. God whispers to us in our pleasures, speaks in our conscience, but shouts in our pains: it is his megaphone to rouse a deaf world."[1] The way we respond to the pain of crisis makes all the difference to how and when we will recover, and how we will respond when the next crisis comes. And it will come, in one form or another. That's an unpleasant fact of life on this planet.

There is a good biblical illustration from the life of David. For some time, David was pursued by King Saul, who wanted to murder him out of jealousy. During this period, David gathered around him a militia of six hundred brave men who traveled and warred with him. Their hub of operation was the town of Ziklag.

One day when David and his men were away from home, an army of Amalekites raided Ziklag, took away all the women and children, and set the city on fire. When David's troops returned, they saw that the enemy had abducted their families and ruined their property. They blamed David and began talking of stoning him to death.

A good-size crisis, I'd say. The danger is clear, of course. But what is the opportunity?

---

1. C.S. Lewis, *The Problem of Pain.* HarperCollins, 2014.

David could have torn his clothes and frozen in a posture of mourning because his own wives and children were missing too. Or he could have run away from his men and hidden in the wilderness alone. But David the warrior, the man after God's heart, "found strength in the LORD his God" (1 Sam. 30:6). He inquired of the Lord, who assured him that he had opportunity to go after his enemies and take everything back. And because the Lord is ever true to his word, this is exactly what happened.

The narrator of the story tells us that when David's men returned from battle, "nothing was missing: young or old, boy or girl, plunder or anything else they [the Amalekites] had taken. David brought everything back" (v. 19). Beyond this, David took so much plunder from the stores of the Amalekites that he sent lavish gifts to his friends and family and friends back at home in Judah. David faced danger courageously and spiritually. He took the opportunity the Lord provided and came out way ahead of where he was when the calamity hit.

David didn't always respond as well to crisis, and sometimes we don't respond so well. Sometimes it's like we're in crashing surf. A powerful wave hits us and tosses us under the water, completely disoriented. Just when we find our footing, another wave comes. Sometimes we can't stand long enough to catch our breath.

But whether we respond quickly or slowly, we can look for a redemptive gift in whatever crisis we face. There is always opportunity for growth hidden in our pain. If we, like David, find our strength in the Lord, even the worst crisis can be an opportunity to grow in grace, wisdom, and patience.

TRYING OR TRAINING

I've learned in my work that in the initial stages of therapy, it is essential to help clients to identify and define their goals for life and let those goals inform the goals for therapy. Much is revealed in the assessment process about the client's worldview, values, history, and temperament, all essential to building a therapeutic understanding. If we skip over this important step, both client and therapist may wind up frustrated or unsatisfied, because neither of us is clear about where we are headed or why. We may have to readjust the coordinates later, but it's good to start with at least a tentative destination in mind.

As I listen to the client's story, I often hear about a set of struggles—with depression, anxiety, relationship dysfunction, spiritual stagnation, or unresolved grief or trauma. Most people tell the same story many times, to themselves and to various people in their lives before they wind up in my office telling it to me. I ask myself, How can I respond in a way that is different and more helpful?

One way I do this is with a wonderful tool I call "reframing." And one of the most common reframes is replacing the language of *trying* with the language of *training*. This idea does not originate with me, of course. Any motivational speaker or coach worth his or her salt knows that while we are in *trying* mode, we are usually spinning our wheels in neutral; we haven't shifted into gear. Training implies action. It gets us moving.

There may be a man who says, "I'm *trying* to be more loving toward my wife, but nothing I do seems to make a difference." Or the grown daughter who says, "I'm *trying* to forgive my dad for his abuse, but how can I when he's never taken responsibility for it?" Or the college student who says, "I'm *trying* to keep up with everything, but every day I still feel overwhelmed with anxiety and worry." Or the mom who says, "I'm *trying* to get back on track with the Lord, but I have no time alone to study or pray!"

Scripture does not tell husbands to *try* to love their wives. It says simply to love them (Eph. 5:25). The Bible does not command us to *try* to forgive others. It says we are to forgive them because we have been forgiven (Luke 6:37; Eph. 4:32). The word does not tell us to *try* not to be anxious; it says, "Don't be anxious" (Phil. 4:6). Scripture does not suggest that we *try* to pursue the Lord, but that he rewards those who "diligently seek him" (Heb. 11:6).

When we don't think we can meet these standards in the Word of God, we sometimes delude ourselves that we gain some wiggle room because while we may not be progressing, at least we are trying really hard. It allows us to procrastinate, chicken out, make excuses, or justify not fulfilling commitments we've made to ourselves, other people, or the Lord.

Moses told the Israelites before they crossed over the Jordan that they were not required to make specific vows to the Lord. But if they chose to make them, there would be severe consequences for not fulfilling them promptly (Deut. 23:21). The same principle applies to us as Christ-followers. We don't *try* to do what we say we are going to do. We do it.

Well, Ruth, you say, what if it feels like there is a huge gap between where I want to be and where I am? What if I don't even know how to begin? Isn't trying better than doing nothing at all? John Ortberg, in his book about spiritual disciplines *The Life You've Always Wanted*, gives a couple of good examples that illustrate the answer: instead of trying, we get into training.

If you wanted to run a marathon, but you'd never been a runner, it would be foolish to say, "I'm going to *try* to run a marathon." No, what you would do is begin training. You'd start by running small distances, gradually increasing the distances until you had conditioned your muscles and cardiovascular system to endure twenty-six miles of running.

Or, if you wanted to play a complex piano concerto but had never touched a piano, you wouldn't say you were going to *try* to play the concerto. You would look for the best teacher to train you in proper technique, music theory, reading music, etc., and you'd practice scales, exercises, and simpler pieces, progressively working up to the skill needed to play one of Bach's or Beethoven's masterpieces.

If loving the people in our lives is difficult, we don't resort to *trying* to do so. This is a failing strategy. But if we accept and submit to God's discipline, we find that he can train us to guard our hearts against bitterness. We can train our mouths not to speak with cruelty or contempt. Holy Spirit can and will guide us into acts of love and kindness. Before we know it, we have changed from the inside out. Loving others has become a trained, conditioned response. When we fail or fall short (and we will at times), we don't quit. We press on with our training in love because it is what God expects of us. No excuses.

Likewise with forgiveness. We can train ourselves to speak prayers of forgiveness toward those who have wronged us, even if we don't feel it yet. Pretty soon we find that this becomes more than mere words; forgiveness has become the foundational ethic that motivates us. We feel healthier and freer because we've purged out the poison of unforgiveness.

In the case of anxiety, we commit and find the support we need to move forward in spite of fear, doing it anyway (whatever *it* is), confronting the things that trigger fear. We train our hearts to be more courageous. And if we are like the mom who is spiritually stuck, we find a new, refreshing way to connect with the Lord and do it for at least twenty-one days until it becomes a new habit. We will have trained ourselves into a state of greater spiritual vitality.

All of these training curricula take time, some a lot and some just a little, depending on the starting place and the size of the goal. All growth and change is a process. But trying is not the method of engagement. We gain ground by submitting to the loving discipline of the Lord, allowing him to train us in love, faith, holiness, and courage.

BUTS AND ANDS

So often in ministry and counseling work I encounter people plagued by "*buts*."

"I'd like to get out and meet some new people, *but…*"

"I'd like to go back to church, *but…*"

"I'd like to tell my husband/wife/mom/dad/son/daughter, etc., how I really feel, *but…*"

"I'd like to quit this bad habit, *but…*"

"I'd like to change jobs, *but…*"

These are just some of the examples I have heard that touch on different aspects of their lives and well-being.

What follows the *but* is often a statement of fear, doubt, or unbelief, such as, "I'm afraid I'll be rejected…I'm afraid they won't understand…I'm afraid of how I'll cope…I'm afraid I'll never be able to find a better job…"

Or worse, it is a statement of shame and self-loathing, such as, "I know no one would want to be with me…I'm too messed up to dare get around a bunch of Christians…I'm worthless…It's hopeless…"

But is a necessary word in our vocabulary. It is a way of expressing a contrast or qualifying a statement. *But,* it can also be a dangerous word. It can shut down growth. It can keep people stuck in depression, loneliness, and defeat.

Sometimes I recognize that someone is *"butting"* themselves to death because I am feeling frustrated. I'm trying to help them find solutions, and everything that we discuss has an obstacle, a *but* that rules it out as a possibility. I'm aware of the *but* syndrome by my own frustration in trying to be helpful.

I've found a way of working through this that comes as a revelation to people when I suggest it. It is to replace their *but* with an *and*." Check out what a difference this makes:

> "I'd like to get out and meet some new people, *and* I acknowledge that this is hard for me."
>
> *Self-acceptance instead of fear of rejection.*

> "I'd like to go back to church, *and* I need to find a community where I will be welcomed as I am."
>
> *A positive goal instead of religious self-condemnation.*

> I'd like to tell _______ how I feel, *and* I need to learn how to express myself more honestly."
>
> *A move toward assertiveness instead of passivity and co-dependency.*

> I'd like to change jobs, *and* I'd better start looking now because it might take time and effort to find it.
>
> *Optimism and determination instead of pessimism and defeatism.*

Scripture actually contains lots of "buts." Do a search and you'll generate hundreds of instances. God contrasts himself with his creation, his ways with the double-minded ways of humanity, his goodness and light with wickedness and darkness. "But" is incredibly useful for that.

We celebrate the places in Scripture and in our lives when God intervenes with a *"but* God." This is where God takes our impossibilities and makes them possibilities, only through his love and power.

Here's a favorite one of these: "But God, who is rich in mercy, because of His great love with which He loved us, even when we were dead in trespasses, made us alive together with Christ" (Eph. 2:4–5, KJV).

But God is the best kind of *but* statement!

But also plays an important part in scriptural admonishments, such as, "When you give to the needy, do not announce it with trumpets, as the hypocrites do…*but* when you give to the needy, do not let your left hand know what your right hand is doing" (Matt. 6:2–3). Or "Do not be unwise but understand what the will of the Lord is" (Eph. 5:17).

Of course, we must take heed to these instructions that include a *but. But,* as illustrated above, in our personal lives *but* can be grossly and destructively overused. Is it possible that Scripture can guide us toward some *ands* that might allow us to be more positive and fruitful? Try on a few:

When wondering how our needs will be met:

> "*And* my God will meet all your needs according to His
> glorious riches in Christ Jesus" (Phil. 4:19).

When afraid because things are not looking so good:

> "*And* we know that in all things God works for the good
> of those who love him, who have been called according
> to His purpose" (Rom. 8:28).

When discouraged because the world seems hopelessly lost:

> "The night is nearly over; the day is almost here. So let us
> put aside the deeds of darkness and put on the armor of
> light" (Rom. 13:12).

And there are many more. As we live our lives and search the Scriptures, the best route is to notice both the *buts* and the *ands,* because we need them both. *And* we can ask the Holy Spirit's help to keep them in balance.

BULLIES AND BABIES

One day I went to counsel two of the men in a ministry where I served. I am always mindful of the Holy Spirit's presence and purpose in these conversations. I have the amazing privilege of witnessing the harmony of Scripture and Spirit and Life as we meet in his presence.

One of these men, I'll call him Jason, spoke of the relentless bullying he suffered as a child. He was small in stature, but not weak, and he learned to fight back against the bullies. They discovered the hard way that it was best to leave him alone because he could quickly flatten them with his fists.

Jason went on to master martial arts, defending himself and other bullied kids. Eventually, though, his learned aggression, combined with drug and alcohol abuse, produced enough rage to ultimately land him in prison. Released a few months ago and living in a safe haven with loving companions, he was undergoing an intense process of life recovery. Our work together centered on recognizing and healing the root causes of his woundedness and abuse and redirecting his energies toward more godly, constructive pursuits. He had resolved to give up fighting with his fists.

I suggested to him that Lord might be uncovering a calling to defend the defenseless as a man of God, in spirit, truth, and righteousness. Having just attended a pro-life rally, I shared this as an example of fighting injustice against the most defenseless, voiceless populations that now exists in our culture. We can take a stand against the sanctioned "bullying" of humans who haven't yet taken their first breaths.

At this point, Jason teared up, telling me of his great tenderness toward babies. Outrage and immense sorrow overtake him any time he hears a news report about injury to a child. I challenged Jason to pray earnestly and listen to God's instruction on using this redemptive gift of compassion toward the defenseless. This is well-grounded in his own suffering, and God never wastes our suffering.

The next day I was reading the book of Exodus. I had goosebumps as I read about the Hebrew midwives who, after Pharaoh's command to kill all the male Hebrew babies, refused to do so because of their fear of God. "So God was kind to the midwives and the people increased and became even more numerous. And because the midwives feared God, he gave them families of their own" (Exod. 1:17, 20–21). It makes sense that midwives would be ardently pro-life, and that God would reward their courage. This was civil disobedience at its best.

As if that were not enough to fill my heart with awe, I read about the rescue of Moses as an infant and his upbringing in the palace of Pharaoh. When grown, Moses developed a tendency to involve himself in conflicts. First, he killed an Egyptian who was abusing a Hebrew slave. Then, when he witnessed a fight between two of his Israelite kinsmen, he attempted to defend the one he considered to be in the right. This Moses was the man who was to become Israel's lawgiver, the rescuer, leader, and defender of an entire nation. This one cast helplessly into the river as an infant on the edict of a bully became a fighter of bullies, an advocate for the vulnerable.

But because his time had not yet come, Moses fled in fear of retribution by the Egyptians. He spent forty years as a herdsman, in a sense "imprisoned" in obscurity and manual labor until the fulfillment of his calling to lead his people out of slavery. His is a story of standing up against bullies, and all enemies of the Lord, in boldness and humility.

I texted Jason and urged him to read this story in which, for him, Scripture comes to life. He could use his past wounds to energize his future choices to defend the defenseless. He could fight for life with the spiritual weapons the Lord provides.

PRACTICING
AND PLAYING

When I was in my undergraduate years I studied music seriously, completing a degree in jazz guitar and vocal performance. That degree, along with a Metro card, will allow you to ride on a New York City subway these days. But I learned a great deal about life through my study of jazz.

Linc Chamberland, a brilliant guitarist and pedagogue, and my teacher for two years, had an especially formative influence on me. Several conversations with Linc from long ago have stayed with me throughout my adult life. One of the most valuable was about the relationship between practicing music and playing it.

During my two-hour lessons, Linc sure put me through my paces! We'd start a song like "Stella By Starlight," tamely executing the chords and melody together in normal 4/4 time in the standard key of B-flat. Then, he'd call out, "OK Ruth, now modulate to the key of G-flat." Or "OK, Ruth, now in 5/4 time."

What?! Now? Just like that? You're kidding, right? No, he was serious. I'd stumble through, feeling like I was on a wickedly devised obstacle course, painfully banging my head or stubbing my toes. It was humiliating at times, and he knew it. But he would just laugh and say, "You don't come here to play, do you? You can play on your own time. I thought you came here to work!"

Linc cautioned me about getting distracted in my practice time at school or home as well. He knew well the temptation to stop running scales, arpeggios, chord cycles, or rhythmic exercises—the tools to build the fundamental skills I was seeking to develop—and to start noodling around and playing tunes. He told me to make sure that when it was practice time, I was really practicing.

But Linc also cautioned me against practicing when it was time to play. When I had a gig, or even an opportunity to jam with friends, I was to let go of my fixation on the technical elements and just create music. He believed that as a player I had my own unique sound and message, and he didn't want me to miss the joy of expressing that. I think that's the best thing Linc taught me: how to practice, and when to let go of practicing and simply play.

There is a useful parallel to other parts of life. Counselors and other professionals often call the work they do with clients a "practice." Why is it called a practice? In my case, I provide a place and context where we talk about fundamental life principles, skill sets, belief systems, and resiliencies that make life more purposeful, peaceable, and joyful. Clients (hopefully) practice them in the scenarios and relationships they face between sessions. As we go, I'm always looking and listening for the day when clients reveal that they have internalized the things we've been "practicing" together and that they've become more wholehearted, free, and alive. They tell me in one way or another that life has begun to offer moments that feel more like playing than practicing. That is the day when I've worked myself out of a job, and I rejoice in that.

We never fully stop the training and practicing process, in music or in life. As disciples, we can always expand our capacity to love God and others the way Jesus does. The spiritual disciplines of prayer, fasting, giving, resting, studying, etc., are tools that help us to develop spiritual health and fitness.

But there is a time to step back and enjoy the fruits of God's constant, sublime grace, allowing ourselves the freedom to play. This is when we notice that we are more joyful than we were yesterday, and we can't explain why. We notice the pink flowers blooming in the middle of February. We express gratitude because although strawberries are not necessary for our survival, there they are to enjoy in all their lusciousness.

We see the amazing, diverse, lush beauty of all that God has created, formed, and made, and we marvel. Our worship overflows. We forget about practicing for a while and let a sweet song flow from our lips or strings. This song reaches the ears of God, and he smiles and taps his feet with pleasure. Maybe he even dances.

8

IN THE WORLD

Being a Christ-follower in the twenty-first-century Western world feels like a minefield sometimes. We hold to an ancient worldview and attempt to remain faithful to a belief system that doesn't match the political and cultural climate in which we live.

It is important to recognize that we are not special or unique in this situation. From the beginning, Christians have faced hostility in every generation, somewhere in the world. Christians have been martyred when they would not renounce their countercultural faith.

In this set of essays, we'll look at teachings of Jesus and his apostles that help us navigate the often dangerous intersection of Christianity and contemporary society. We'll learn from the Old Testament examples of Daniel and Jehu as they confronted the ungodly, pagan practices surrounding them. Finally, we'll imagine how the world would be different if Christ had never established his church and kingdom on the earth.

SHEEP AMONG WOLVES

"I am sending you out like sheep among wolves. Therefore,
be as shrewd as snakes and as innocent as doves."

MATT. 10:16

Averse like this one, so rich in imagery and depth, warrants digging deeper for meaning, especially when it's something Jesus said.

Jesus sent his twelve disciples on a short-term mission trip to some towns in the Galilee region. They were to take nothing with them—no money, no change of clothes, no itinerary. They were to enter each town and knock on some doors. They were to accept hospitality from the first person who offered it and bless that home by letting their peace rest there. When they encountered hostility, Jesus instructed them, "Shake the dust off your feet when you leave that home or town" (Matt. 10:14).

This assignment is amazing from a modern, Western perspective. Do you know any missionaries or church leaders who would set out on a trip with no luggage, no money or credit cards, no schedule, no clear strategy, and no host organization or family to greet them at their destination? That's a crazy way to do missions, right? According to the story, it was Jesus's way to do missions. He sent his closest friends out, as vulnerable as lambs going into a pack of wolves, without even a change. Without even a change of underwear.

Sheep are prey animals. They are defenseless. They can't fight, so they can only flee or huddle together when threatened. A veterinary manual for sheep farmers points out that sheep become quite anxious and agitated if they become separated from the flock. Farmers who want to keep their sheep healthy are careful that they keep the flock together.[1] Jesus's little flock was to leave the safety of his pastoral care and venture out in the wide world on their own. At least there were twelve of them.

Jesus told them they would run into wolves, maybe a lot of wolves. Wolves are predators who are known for attacking domestic animals like sheep. They do this because it is instinctual: it is in their nature. They also live in packs. When given the opportunity, a pack of wolves will attack a sheep, especially if the sheep wanders from its flock. This explains why Jesus says a good shepherd leaves the flock unguarded to find the one sheep that wanders away—that sheep wouldn't stand a chance in the wilderness alone.

Although Jesus compared his disciples to sheep, he expected them to be as shrewd, prudent, smart, clever, or cunning (in various translations) as snakes when they encountered the wolves. It's a bit puzzling to consider how a sheep can adapt to thinking like a snake.

In Genesis 3:1 we read that the serpent was more subtle (crafty, intelligent, clever, cunning) than all other creatures. I don't know how smart snakes really are, but I do know that that they slither on the ground, and they are agile, which makes them good at escaping danger quickly. Most don't attack unless provoked. Some produce lethal venom that defends them against predators if they do confront one.

We've established that sheep are not agile, intelligent, or able to care for themselves apart from their flock and their shepherd. Could Jesus be saying that we are to continue to identify as his sheep, while learning how to stay safe and whole when facing threats from hostile people? We are not to *call attention* to ourselves but are to be a bit stealthy in our approach. As I've heard our prison chaplain say sternly, "Don't ever get too comfortable here." We must have our eyes open and be ready to respond safely and appropriately in unfamiliar and potentially dangerous environments. And we must also discern when it's time to get out.

When we are spreading the gospel of the kingdom, we are to remain as harmless, inoffensive, and innocent as doves. What do we

---

1. Social Behavior of Sheep - Behavior - Merck Veterinary Manual (merckvetmanual.com)

Flock of Sheep, South New Zealand, photo by Andrea Lightfoot

know about doves? From an online source called "SpiritualRay" we learn how doves have come to be associated with peace and innocence. Doves often build nests in proximity to people. When observed, it becomes clear that they mate for life and are diligent parents to their hatchlings. And just as Jesus suggests, they are harmless creatures, eating only vegetation for their sustenance.[1]

In summary, we are sheep who will encounter wolves. When we do, we are to be as shrewd as serpents and as harmless as doves. To do this, we must: a) stay connected to Jesus and his flock; b) be agile and wise in our handling of the gospel among those who do not yet believe; c) accept that we will encounter opposition and prepare ourselves; and d) never harm anyone.

We don't bite people and inject venom. We are to be gentle, loving, and loyal, as much as we are able. When people reject us and our message, Jesus gives us permission to depart with no regrets. We bring no reproach to the name or cause of Jesus Christ.

---

1. "This Is the Story of Why the Dove Is a Symbol of Peace and Love," SpiritualRay, https://spiritualray.com/why-is-dove-symbol-of-peace-love.

DANIEL'S TESTS
AND OURS, PART 1:
PURITY, KNOWLEDGE,
AND WORSHIP

The stories of the early chapters of the book of Daniel are captivating in plot, character, action, and scope. Lovers of God over the centuries have taken encouragement from the example set by Daniel, Shadrach, Meshach, and Abednego. These servants of the God of Israel faced numerous challenges to their holy, character-driven choices in a pagan culture. I have observed six tests put to these Hebrew youth that proved they were true and blameless followers of the one true God. This has obvious application to our own lives in this twenty-first-century world.

Daniel and his three friends were among those exiled to Babylon when King Nebuchadnezzar seized control of Jerusalem. They had been members of the Israelite royal court, the cream of the crop, "young men without any physical defect, handsome, showing aptitude for every kind of learning, well-informed, quick to understand, qualified to serve in the king's palace" (1:4). Upon arrival in this strange new land, they received training for three years in all aspects of Babylonian language and culture to further prepare them for service.

What no one realized at that point was that the God they served was about to guide them through several significant tests. Their responses to these tests under severe pressure and persecution would confirm their qualification to be more than mere bureaucrats in Nebuchadnezzar's empire. Refined like pure gold, they proved themselves fit for noble use in the kingdom of Almighty God. Daniel, Shadrach, Meshach, and Abednego were tested in six areas: purity, spiritual knowledge, worship, speaking truth, integrity, and discipline. We will examine these in more detail and identify the corresponding tests we face in our times.

Daniel's Test of Purity. Nebuchadnezzar expected the Hebrew immigrants to conform to Babylonian culture and royal lifestyle, including their diet. Daniel, in his heart, "resolved not to defile himself with the royal food and wine" (1:8). The king's servant agreed to allow ten days to see if after consuming a plainer diet of vegetables and water, Daniel and his Hebrew friends would look less healthy than the pagan boys. The result was that they looked quite hearty after ten days, so the servant granted permission for them to keep to this regimen.

The text doesn't reveal the reason for their self-imposed dietary restrictions, so we can't know exactly. But we do know that Daniel believed that this was essential to protect them from defilement, and that is enough. He trusted that God would help them to maintain their purity, and he did.

Our Test of Purity. Many people inside and outside the church have strong ideas about food, what we should and should not eat, and why. While diet is a crucial aspect of the stewardship of our bodies, this is not necessarily a primary test of our purity as it was for Daniel. As New Testament believers, we are not bound by religious dietary restrictions. Jesus (and, later, Peter and Paul) confirmed that purity is a matter of the heart, and not dependent on what we eat.

What, then, are the elements of contemporary Western culture that compromise and interfere with our purity before God? Mostly, it is what we see and hear that is blatantly or subtly immoral, corrupt, or perverse. We can become so desensitized to profanity, barbarity, violence, and pornography that we don't even realize it may be defiling us.

When we experience spiritual conviction to turn away from this kind of content, are we not being tested in our desire for purity? Doesn't everyone watch and listen to these things and talk about them when they get together socially? Are we willing to face exclusion from parts of the cultural conversation? Daniel didn't seem to care about that. His priority was to stand before God with no shame.

Daniel's Test of Spiritual Knowledge. King Nebuchadnezzar had an unsettling dream he wanted interpreted. He demanded that the magicians and wise men not only interpret the dream but tell the dream itself, which they deemed impossible. When the king didn't get his way, he became enraged and threatened to kill all of his advisers if they couldn't give him an answer.

Daniel heard of this and implored his three friends to pray with him, asking "for mercy from the God of heaven concerning this mystery" (2:18) to spare their lives. Daniel received revelation of both the dream and its interpretation. Daniel passed the test, trusting Almighty God to give the knowledge and understanding necessary to accomplish an assignment deemed impossible by the wise men of the day.

Our Test of Spiritual Knowledge. If we desire to influence others for Christ, we must pray, as Daniel did, that the Lord would give us spiritual discernment and wisdom. We often look to the wrong sources of information. We trust worldly voices and sources with greedy motives, people who covet power more than truth. When under pressure, we must turn to the Spirit of God and the Word of God for wisdom and knowledge. Trusting God to give us the revelation we need may not be the easy way, but it is the right way. That's why it is a test.

Their Test of Worship. This story features Daniel's friends, Shadrach, Meshach, and Abednego. King Nebuchadnezzar erected a gargantuan likeness of himself. He commanded that whenever any kind of music was heard in the land, all citizens must bow down and worship the statue. Shadrach, Meshach, and Abednego adamantly refused. Their courageous civil disobedience and unwavering trust in God incited the king to order them thrown into a furnace so hot that it burned up the soldiers escorting them. Strangely, they were completely unharmed. They passed the test of rejecting idolatry and worshipping only Almighty God, and he rewarded their devotion.

Our Test of Worship. Shadrach, Meshach, and Abednego trusted that God would rescue them from the flames if they reserved their worship only for him. They went even further, declaring that even if he chose not to rescue them, they weren't going to bow down to any idol. This is a courageous choice that God promises to bless.

Temptation and testing in this area are ubiquitous but can be subtle enough that even mature believers are deceived. We may not bow down to statues, but don't we often divide our affection for God with so many other loves in our lives—possessions, activities, ministries, relationships, entertainments? Doesn't he often get a paltry share of our time and devotion? Aren't we tested daily to choose worshipping God when surrounded by an array of other colorful, shiny options?

DANIEL'S TESTS AND OURS, PART 2: TRUTH, INTEGRITY, AND DISCIPLINE

Daniel's Test of Speaking Truth. Nebuchadnezzar had another troubling dream, and this time he knew to call Daniel immediately. To Daniel's dismay, the interpretation God gave him was extremely unfavorable to the king. The dream prophesied that the king would lose his sanity and wander in the wilderness like a beast.

This tyrant was known to kill servants for any reason or no reason. Daniel could have left things out or watered down the clear message of the dream. With respect and humility, Daniel shared God's revelation fully and clearly. Daniel passed the test of the prophet, at the risk of his life. Daniel's words came true precisely, and once Nebuchadnezzar's sanity was restored, he too praised Almighty God.

Our Test of Speaking Truth. In America, we are living through a time when the right to free speech, especially for people of faith, is at great risk. Only certain political and social opinions are deemed acceptable in the cultural conversation. Daniel's story shows us that this is not a new experience for followers of the God of the Bible. There are few who boldly, publicly proclaim a biblical faith if it subjects them to the contempt of the elites or the masses. But if more of us would do it, we might see our witness for Christ rise all the way to the highest places of leadership. Like Daniel, we might influence those in power to overcome their pride and bow down before God.

Daniel's Test of Integrity. Belshazzar was in some ways more perverse and despicable than his predecessor Nebuchadnezzar. He was drunkenly feasting when a disembodied hand appeared and wrote a cryptic message on the palace wall. He called for Daniel and tried to flatter him, promising that he would be "clothed in purple and have a gold chain placed around his neck, and…made the third-highest ruler in the kingdom" (5:7) if Daniel could read the message. Daniel again spoke truth to power and declined the king's gifts, saying, "You may keep your gifts for yourself and give your rewards to someone else" (5:17). Daniel passed the test, not giving in to the temptation to seek wealth, power, or fame at the cost of his integrity. Those who speak for God must not have a price on their integrity.

Our Tests of Integrity. It is not wrong to accept compensation or reward for our service to God. But if we are to truly live as Christ's disciples, we must be content to require nothing but the knowledge that we are faithfully executing his assignment. This is a very personal test; it goes right to the heart of our devotion to Christ and our secure identity in him.

We follow the ways of Christ whether anyone is watching or rewarding us for it. To pass the many tests of integrity that come, we must never look for moral shortcuts, intentionally deceive or cheat, or make excuses when we fall short of God's standards. We don't exploit others for our own gain. This testing happens nearly every day, throughout our entire lives.

Daniel's Test of Discipline. Daniel kept the holy habit of praying to God three times a day. Knowing this, jealous rivals on the king's staff convinced the king to forbid prayer to anyone but himself. The consequence for disobeying this order was to become supper for the lions. Daniel, hearing this, went to his room and prayed as usual. When soldiers threw him into the lions' den, the lions did him no harm. He testified, "My God sent his angel, and shut the mouth of the lions. They have not harmed me, for I was found innocent in his sight" (6:22). Daniel passed the test, keeping his spiritual disciplines in place even under threat of death.

Our Test of Discipline. There are as many ways to practice spiritual disciplines as there are worshippers. The test here is to be consistent and diligent in whatever personal convictions we hold. What do we need to maintain our intimacy with Christ? What will cause us to grow and bear fruit? For some disciples, it may be simple and unstructured. Others thrive with more structure. We aren't to judge one another's choices regarding these disciplines. But we are to honor God daily with our own.

Our tests are not new. They just appear in our generation with new characters, fancier technologies, and updated plot lines. Jesus told us we would be tested as he was. His people rejected him and executed him on a tree without a proper trial. He told his disciples that people would hate them just for being his followers, and this is still often true today.

Our test is whether we will walk faithfully in his ways and speak very clearly and publicly on matters that are important to God, even if it puts us at risk of harm. We represent his kingdom and gospel, whatever the consequences. We use our voices with courage, knowing that the truth and power of Jesus are working through us.

HOW CAN
THERE BE PEACE?

When Joram saw Jehu he asked, "Have you come in peace,
Jehu?" "How can there be peace," Jehu replied, "as long as all
the idolatry and witchcraft of your mother, Jezebel, abound?"

2 KINGS 9:22

The biblical stories of kingship succession in Judah and Israel are not pretty, but replete with political intrigue, generational curses, murder, warfare, and betrayal. Reading these narratives, I can't help relating them to the current state of things in America. In this story, Scripture comes to life to guide us into the truth about our spiritual condition.

The Lord commanded one of the young protégés of the prophet Elisha to anoint a man named Jehu as king over Israel. This happened while Joram, son of the evil Ahab, was still on Israel's throne. After the anointing ceremony, Jehu made his way to the palace where King Joram was recuperating from wounds of battle. Judah's King Ahaziah was there visiting him. This is significant because the righteous kings of Judah typically avoided alliances with the wicked kings of Israel, but Ahaziah was clearly not one of the righteous ones. It appears he and Joram were cronies. Ahaziah had become as morally compromised and idolatrous as Joram.

Jehu's mission was to seize the kingship from Joram and, in the process, to kill every remaining relative of King Ahab. The watchman on the roof of Joram's palace alerted the king that someone was coming across the plains of Jezreel with horses and chariots. Joram dispatched a messenger to ask the reckless rider if he came in peace. Jehu's response was, "What do you know about peace? Fall in behind me!" (2 Kings 9:18) The messenger didn't return, so Joram sent another, and Jehu gave him the same answer (v.19). The second messenger didn't return either, so Joram climbed into his own chariot to meet Jehu face to face, man to man.

When Joram approached he asked, "Have you come in peace, Jehu?" Jehu answered his question with another question: ""How can there be peace as long as all the idolatry and witchcraft of your mother, Jezebel, abound?" (v.22) This question stops me in my tracks and prompts me to look around the landscape of life in America in the early twenty-first century.

We keep hearing about how divided we are as a nation. On the surface, it is a political divide. People who support the current administration versus people who despise it and want to take it down. Dig a little bit deeper and it looks like a culture war—people who are not able to get along because they differ sharply in their values and worldviews. But at the depth, at its roots, it is entirely spiritual. It is rooted not in differing ideologies, but in shared idolatries.

How can there be peace when millions of American babies are aborted every year, like babies were sacrificed to the god Molech? How can there be peace when sexual confusion and perversion are rampant as in Sodom? How can there be peace when thousands practice violence like the depraved citizens of Nineveh?

How can there be peace when people seethe with hatred for those who hold different beliefs, like so many of the political operatives in the days of the prophets? How can there be peace when so many bow at altars of greed and materialism, and others lust for power at the expense of the weak and vulnerable? How can there be peace when so-called journalists disseminate deceptive propaganda on every side?

American culture is in the spiritual grip of Jezebel, the queen who represents the killing and persecution of God's righteous servants. She who despises everything good, pure, innocent, and wholesome. This is the spirit that tugs at peoples' natural appetites, pulling them into addiction, insanity, depravity, and bondage. How can there be peace?

Only with repentance and revival of hearts. Only with the freedom the gospel of the kingdom brings into the world. We need leaders who will tear down altars of secularism, especially when they've been fashioned within the walls of our churches. We need lovers of his Word and doers of his Word, without apology. We need an army of peacemakers who feed the poor, visit the prisoners, and speak words of life. We need prophets and intercessors who will war faithfully in the Spirit on behalf of those in bondage. We need people like Jesus who walk in his authority and his deep compassion.

UPSIDE DOWN AND RIGHT SIDE UP

Anyone who has studied the gospel of Jesus Christ—and especially those of us who have been trying to live it out—have learned this: Jesus doesn't measure things the same way the world does. Not success, power, wealth, honor, justice, sin, forgiveness, or even love.

Sometimes it seems an upside-down gospel because Jesus's way is opposite, the inverse of the world's way. I'd prefer to think that the world's way is upside down, and Jesus's way sets it right for those who dare to believe it. It is a way of being in the world without conforming to it.

I have a couple of biblical examples of these inverted realities. The first is Jesus's parable of the vineyard owner who hires workers to harvest the grapes. He employs a crew very early in the morning and promises them a certain wage for the day's work. At nine, noon, three p.m., and again at five p.m., when he finds men standing idle in the street, he sends them out to join the rest. At day's end, they all line up to receive their wages, and are all paid the same amount. Outrageous, right?

We are well conditioned to the way the world measures fairness. We hold it to be self-evident that our reward should always be proportional to the measure of time, effort, or talent we have invested. The workers who began their workday before the sun came up cried, "These who were hired last worked only one hour, and you have made them equal to us who have borne the burden of the work and the heat of the day" (Matt. 20:12).

Is Jesus unjust? Would you hire him as your union negotiator? No, of course Jesus is not unjust. He is the only one who always judges rightly.

Jesus says that it is the master's prerogative how he wants to deal with his servants. Those who arrive early are blessed in doing so. Those who arrive late are equally blessed for showing up. It is not about how long we've been part of the work—it is that God has welcomed us into his vineyard at all. God's sovereignty in our salvation is a key principle in the kingdom of God. Sinners, tax collectors, and late-comers to the party still get to eat at the Master's table. This is only unfair when judged by a worldly, religious spirit.

The second is Jesus's parable of the two servants. The first owes his master a huge sum of money. When the master tries to collect, the servant falls at his feet and begs him to forgive the debt, and he does. This servant goes out and finds another servant who owes him a small debt. He demands that his fellow servant pay up, or he will send him to debtor's prison. The master hears of this, and calls the first servant in. He reprimands him severely, saying, "You wicked servant, I canceled all that debt of yours because you begged me to. Shouldn't you have had mercy on your fellow servant just as I had on you?" (Matt. 18:32–33). The master sent this servant to prison until he could sell everything he owned and repay the debt.

This parable makes clear that it is not the size of the debt that is of concern to the Lord, but the command to forgive. His forgiveness of our incalculable sin debt makes it a bit ridiculous that we would not be willing to forgive those who owe us something. God's mercy toward us is a key principle in the kingdom of God, and it compels us to forgive one another, whatever the size of the debt. Those forgiven much are often those who love and forgive the most (Luke 7:47). This is only illogical when judged by a worldly, hard-hearted spirit.

The Bible is replete with examples of this upside-down and right-side dichotomy. Our faith and courage are bolstered when we remember that Jesus knows we are living in an upside-down world. We also become more alert and consistent in our pursuit of the truth that turns us right-side up.

IDENTITY POLITICS DON'T WORK IN THE KINGDOM OF GOD

It's easy to get sucked into the very negative media news cycle. To counter this, I find it necessary and beneficial to daily focus on Scripture, worship, and what I sense the Spirit is saying. But there is no denying or avoiding the fact that the political and social landscape is has become quite ugly. To understand how the larger social picture should or should not impact us and our spheres of influence, we must refer to the eternal, reliable sources of knowledge and wisdom.

There is a prevailing hostility and divisiveness in our culture. People are aligning with and separating themselves from others according to some aspect of their identity—skin color, ethnicity, language, religion, age, gender, sexual preference, or some "intersectionality" of these characteristics. Their specialness allegedly entitles them to a benefit, accommodation, or influence upon social policy, with little regard for how their demands impact society as a whole. The pundits call this "identity politics." It is "us-and-them-ism," to coin a phrase.

The Bible speaks of this social phenomenon in many places. In his letter to the Philippians, the apostle Paul lists the markers of his identity, his specialness. He was "circumcised on the eighth day, of the people of Israel, of the tribe of Benjamin, a Hebrew of Hebrews; in regard to the law, a Pharisee; as for zeal, persecuting the church; as for righteousness based on the law, faultless" (Phil. 3:5–6). For a

Jew of his day, he had an outstanding pedigree. It set him apart from others who were not like him—not from his tribe, not as religious, not as educated, not as zealous, not as righteous.

But instead of boasting about or standing upon these markers of his status, Paul remarkably calls it all a big pile of dung, or garbage, or manure, or worthless trash, depending on what translation we read.

Before his conversion, Saul (later called Paul) was a zealous Pharisee, a self-righteous defender of the Law of Moses and rabbinic tradition. He was viciously pursuing followers of the Way, determined to put a stop to the gospel message that was spreading like a virus throughout the Roman Empire. He saw Christians as a threat to his own beliefs and way of living (sound familiar?), so he wanted to snuff them out.

But something happened along the way. He encountered the risen Christ himself. Supernaturally bounced off his horse and struck blind for three days, he was led by his companions to a house nearby. God sent a disciple named Ananias to lay hands on Paul, restore his sight, and introduce him to his new calling as an apostle of Christ.

After this, Paul tore up his résumé. His Jewishness didn't count for a thing anymore. His training with the rabbis only mattered to the extent that he could cite Scriptures proving that Jesus Christ was the Messiah. Paul decided to become "all things to all men" (1 Cor. 9:22). This required a letting go of any aspect of his identity that would close him off from those in need of the gospel.

He went first to the Jews whenever he had the chance, because they were his people. When in a new town on his missionary journeys, he taught first in the synagogues. But he soon realized that God had commissioned him to bring the good news to the Gentiles. In Pisidia of Antioch, he rebuked the unbelieving Jews, saying, "We had to speak the word of God to you first. Since you reject it and do not consider yourselves worthy of eternal life, we now turn to the Gentiles" (Acts 13:46). Before encountering Jesus, he wouldn't have considered defiling himself by keeping company with Gentiles.

At the same time, another famous apostle named Peter was experiencing his own turning point. While entranced in prayer on a rooftop, the Lord showed him a vision of all sorts of creatures considered unclean for Jews to eat, commanding Peter to kill and eat them. Peter protested, defending his religious purity. The Lord's message to Peter was, "Do not call anything impure that God has made clean" (Acts 10:15). Understandably puzzled, Peter did not have to wait long for understanding of the relevance of his vision.

Messengers knocked on the door, summoning Peter to minister to a Gentile centurion and his household. When they readily received the word and the Spirit, Peter reported to his friends, "I now realize how true it is that God does not show favoritism" (Acts 10:34). He realized it was not up to him to determine who deserves to hear the truth. Everyone does.

God does not show favoritism, or as the King James translates it, he is "not a respecter of persons." In the world's system, all the things that make us appear different to one another somehow justify our hostility and defensiveness. But these attitudes are invalid in the kingdom of our Lord. God doesn't play the game of identity politics. God stands alone, exalted and perfect. And as the preachers say, we all stand on the same level ground at the foot of the cross.

To be imitators of our Lord and God, we mustn't play favorites either. We must love without partiality, without hypocrisy (James 2:1–9; Rom. 12:9, 18), those who are like us and those who are unlike us. It is only our love for our God that sets us apart as one family from every tongue, tribe, and nation.

> So in Christ Jesus you are all children of God through faith, for all of you who were baptized into Christ have clothed yourselves with Christ. There is neither Jew nor Gentile, neither slave nor free, nor is there male and female, for you are all one in Christ Jesus." (Gal. 3:26–28)

A WORLD WITH NO CHRISTIANS IN IT

Many in our world these days would like to silence Christians or get rid of them entirely. Some are Islamic or other religious fundamentalists who see Christianity as a threat to their power or influence, like the Pharisees or Romans in Jesus's day. Others find the exclusivity claims of the gospel offensive, especially Jesus's declaration that he is "the way, the truth, and the life" and the only way to gain access to the Father (John 14:6).

Still others don't like the evangelical conviction that the truths and moral principles of the Bible should influence behavior and choices in life. They believe it's just a book among many books, and not worthy of special attention in an information-saturated culture. As I was pondering this, I imagined how the world, and the whole course of history, would be different if the Christian church had never come to be.

Jesus is the head of his church. He was quite clear that he wanted his apostles to spread his gospel everywhere, and he made provision by sending his Spirit to direct this momentous task. It worked. While there still may be some people groups that have no Christians among them, their number is shrinking daily due to the power of communication technology. Wherever the gospel is taught accurately, a portion of those who hear it will believe, and some will not. That's how it has been from the beginning.

The gospel of Jesus Christ changes individuals, families, cities, nations, whole civilizations. Devotion to Jesus Christ has inspired countless symphonies and songs, architectural masterpieces, paintings, and sculptures. The founders of the Constitution of the United States of America built it upon their faith in an unchangeable, uncreated Creator who endows the "inalienable" rights we enjoy.

How many hospitals would never have been built without the compassion of Christ burning in the hearts of his followers? What about universities, scientific discoveries, and libraries full of scholarly work—all birthed from a God-ordained hunger to understand life and creation? Isaac Newton held an absolute belief in the authenticity of the Scriptures and in the existence and lordship of an all-wise God.

Skeptics and atheists often claim that their morality is based in their innate sense of what is good and right. They may feel they are morally superior to most people and don't need to subscribe to a religious or divine moral code. They suppose that when given the choice between serving their own interests and serving the interests of others, they will choose the generous, self-sacrificial path because they are just better than most people. But I believe—and the Bible backs me up—that most humans will *not* do this when the pressure is on, and their lives are at stake.

There are exceptions, of course, when there is a cause big enough to inspire self-sacrifice. The most notable example is World War II, during which the cause of saving the world from fascist domination inspired true heroism. I honor highly and would never minimize the price paid by those who fight selflessly on behalf of others, whatever their underlying motivation or belief system. But for much of the history of the last two thousand years, there is no other story that competes with the gospel of Christ to inspire creativity, courage, generosity, and self-sacrifice.

Not everyone will embrace the way of Jesus. He stated as much. The weeds grow up with the wheat. The goats live among the sheep. There is a broad way that most people take, and it leads to destruction. He said that very few find the narrow way that leads to life (Matt. 7:13–14). I wish this were not true, but it's in the red letters: the words of our Lord.

The scariest thing for me is imagining a world in which no one chooses to love Christ. I picture an unspeakably dark, cruel, unbearable place, with the light of God snuffed out. Jesus declared himself and his followers the light of the world. I take this to mean that without the presence of Christ living in and through his people, the earth would be shrouded in deep darkness.

If Christ and his gospel offend, I can't compel people to feel otherwise. They have a right to their position. And they may think me a fool for believing as I do. But I would suggest that whether they believe it or not, it is because of what Christ and his gospel have wrought that they have light to find their way, even to their very different view.

9

IN TROUBLE AND SUFFERING

> *"I have told you these things, so that in me you may
> have peace. In this world you will have trouble.
> But take heart! I have overcome the world."*
>
> JOHN 16:33.

Suffering has always been and will always be part of the human experience. Life is difficult even from birth when we fight our way out of the womb. None of us get through childhood without some scars and broken places in our bodies and souls. We continue to be tested, tempted, and tried throughout the whole span of our development. We all suffer loss, hardship, loneliness, struggle, and grief; it only varies in degree, and in how we respond to it.

Fortunately for Christ-followers, we have access to a book that teaches us the meaning in some of our suffering and teaches us to grow in faith and resiliency in the face of life's difficulties. The Bible is full of stories, poems, letters, and prophecies that provide wisdom and comfort to sufferers.

In this chapter, we'll look at the nature of crisis and explore the difference between testing and temptation. We'll dig deep into grief and how we can help each other to grieve well. We'll look at the frustration of feeling that God, for an unknown reason, has not heard or answered our prayers for deliverance. We'll see that it is often the stories we tell about our difficulties that make all the difference in how we respond and heal.

IT'S A LONELY
ROAD SOMETIMES

Recently I was talking and praying with a young woman who comes from a ministry and missionary family, and who is a missionary herself. We spoke of the experience of being misunderstood and rejected because of our faith. This can cause a feeling of loneliness and may tempt us to keep quiet and inconspicuous to avoid the risk of rejection or harassment. Suddenly I began thinking about John the Baptist and what it might have been like to see life through his eyes.

John was a very unusual character. He wore a camel-hair tunic, not the fashion of the day, and ate bugs with honey—not the typical diet for a Jew in Israel. He lived alone out in the wilderness. Can you picture him next to a campfire, sleeping on the ground?

John's message of the coming kingdom drew many but repelled many others. He boldly confronted sin, selfishness, and complacency, calling the Pharisees and Sadducees vipers and hypocrites; this must not have scored a lot of points with the religious elites. He cautioned the people about their need for repentance and about the coming fiery baptism of the Holy Spirit. He got in the face of Herod and called out his adultery, an act that eventually cost him his life.

John knew his God-ordained role: to prepare the way for the Messiah, his own cousin Jesus. He knew that when Jesus came fully into his ministry his own ministry would decrease, and he accepted this fact. Like the prophets before him, he faithfully delivered the words

God gave him, suffering persecution, rejection, banishment, imprisonment, and death.

Jesus understood and accepted the unique greatness and purpose of John, but he saw the bigger picture, saying that "the one who is least in the kingdom of heaven is greater than he" (Matt. 11:11). John was just a man. He was God's man, filled with the Spirit, and given the honor of baptizing and then introducing the Lamb of God to the waiting world. But he was destined to exit the story soon after.

I wonder if John got lonely. I wonder if he had any friends he could talk with after a long day of ministry. John could have used a really good dog by his side.

I'll often think about John the Baptist now when people tell me stories about their struggles in ministry. He is worthy of our admiration and emulation for his strength of character and his determination to complete his unique assignment with dignity. It must have been a very lonely road sometimes. When we experience our own moments of loneliness as Jesus-followers, we know we are in the greatest of company. Loneliness is one of many stones on the path of following and representing Jesus.

TEMPTATION
AND TESTING

Does God tempt people to sin? Of course not. James states it explicitly: "When tempted, no one should say, 'God is tempting me.' For God cannot be tempted by evil, nor does he tempt anyone" (James 1:13). But does God test his people? Yes.

If you are reacting negatively to this statement, consider this: The Holy Spirit led Jesus into the wilderness (Matt. 4:1) to undergo a severe round of testing. Scripture indicates that the purpose was to be tempted—or tested, in some translations—by the devil. Before Jesus started his ministry, he was required to hear and then reject the doctrines and manipulations of the devil.

Jesus was perfect in righteousness and holiness. So why this test? Hebrews tells us that it was necessary for our redemption and for our atonement. Jesus was completely a human being and completely a supernatural being. He wasn't a hybrid of God and man, but the perfect representation of both.

> He had to be made like them, fully human in every way, in order that he might become a merciful and faithful high priest in service to God, and that he might make atonement for the sins of the people. *Because he himself suffered when he was tempted, he is able to help those who are being tempted.* (Heb. 2:17–18, emphasis added)

The author later elaborates:

> Therefore, since we have a great high priest who has ascended into heaven, Jesus the Son of God, let us hold firmly to the faith we profess. For we do not have a high priest who is unable to empathize with our weaknesses, but *we have one who has been tempted in every way, just as we are—yet he did not sin.* (Heb. 4:14–15, emphasis added)

If the Spirit of God led Jesus right into this—forty days of fasting and then, in his weakened physical state, withstanding a theological challenge by the subtlest of creatures—why would we assume that we will never have to endure times of testing? We are certainly more in need of refinement and strengthening of our faith and knowledge of God than Jesus ever was.

Jesus countered every argument of the devil with his identity as the Son of God, his complete loyalty to the Father, and his thorough knowledge of the Scriptures. As they were at his baptism, the Father and the Spirit were with him in the wilderness. The devil was no match for them. If he weren't such an evil, conniving liar, I'd almost feel sorry for him. Almost.

If we are true disciples, he tests us because he loves us. Testing is part of discipline, and disciples are those who readily submit to his training and discipline. When we take a class, how is our progress assessed? Usually with a test. The way we approach the test demonstrates whether we have mastered the material. What a tremendous advantage we have with our Father protecting, our Jesus teaching, and the Spirit helping us remember and apply the material!

Before we are well-grounded in the ways of God, we are easily tempted, when we are "dragged away by [our] own evil desire and enticed" (James 1:14). But when we have learned to follow him closely and tests and temptations come, we "approach God's throne of grace with confidence, so that we may receive mercy and find grace to help us in our time of need" (Heb. 4:16).

We may go through times of testing, as Job did, when we can't seem to find him. Job lamented in a particularly painful moment:

"…If I go to the east, he is not there; if I go to the west,
I do not find him. When he is at work in the north, I
do not see him; when he turns to the south, I catch no
glimpse of him. But he knows the way that I take; when
he has tested me, I will come forth as gold." (Job 23:8–10)

I love Job's faith here. He can't see God helping him in his hour
of testing and trouble. But he remains confident that God's watchful
eye is upon him. There will be an end to his struggle. God is doing
a refining work in him that will bring great glory!

Let's not be the kind of Christians who expect everything to be
easy. That's childish faith. Let's embrace the hard stuff as the way that
God is cooking and buffing away the impurities and tarnish so that
the gold within can shine for him. Jesus showed us the way, and he
is with us, even when we don't see him clearly.

GRACE AND
THE THORN

In a deep conversation with a small group of women friends, we were each sharing current life circumstances that bring on the temptation to be afraid. Many of these surrounded family relationships. There was an adoption story, a foster mothering story, marriage stories, toddler stories, and stories of adult children who make one poor decision after another. One friend remarked that she is keenly aware of an extra measure of grace in her life to manage situations that would otherwise seem impossible. I began thinking about Paul's thorn in the flesh.

Many have advanced hypotheses about what afflicted Paul. He didn't reveal it, and I believe there may be a good reason for keeping it hidden from us. It suggests that if he had revealed the exact nature of his chronic irritant, readers might not see the deeper relevance of the text or its application. If he wrote that he had gout, or warts, or migraine headaches, or eye problems (as many people guess), those of us who have never experienced those particular afflictions might get distracted from his real message or fail to apply it.

God's message to and through Paul has a few aspects. One is that sometimes we don't get the answer we think we want or need, even after praying over it several (or one thousand) times. We can't boss God around!

Paul had been through so much in his ministry, from great surges of revelation and triumphant power to days on end of hardship and rejection. He had learned, as he wrote to the Philippians, "the secret of being content in any and every situation" (Phil. 4:12). Paul had surrendered his life to God's mission to the extent that he didn't attribute the lack of removal of the thorn as a judgment from God. This requires maturity in the Lord—to cling to the knowledge of God's goodness even when the thorn remains.

Second, sometimes God does seem to allow his children to struggle with difficulties as he teaches and disciplines them. Many don't like this thought, and it does arouse theological controversy. Paul wrote that the affliction was sent as "a messenger of Satan" to bring torment. Why did God allow this? Paul was God's apostle and faithful servant. Paul's answer was that it was to keep him from becoming conceited because of the abundance of revelation given to him. God allowed Paul to experience demonic torment to keep him humble? That appears to be Paul's perspective.

Our covenant with God does not stipulate that we will never have to fight demonic forces. In fact, Jesus makes clear that advancing his kingdom includes frequently confronting demons. God doesn't send demons to torment us. But neither does he prevent us from experiencing some of their troublemaking in our lives. We can trust that if God is allowing it, he has a reason, whether we understand it or not.

It is a legitimate response to seek freedom and deliverance as soon as possible when we are suffering. But we can also choose to remain alert to the opportunity to grow in character and discipline through our suffering. The Christian walk requires perseverance most when the road is most difficult. Or when a proverbial or literal thorn is causing throbbing pain.

God did not deliver Paul of this thorn, after thrice praying. Instead, Paul heard, "My grace is sufficient for you, for my power is made perfect in weakness" (2 Cor. 12:8). Grace is sufficient. God's power shows up perfectly when we acknowledge our dependence upon him.

When we are weak, he is strong. And when we are even weaker, he is even stronger. Grace fills in the gaps between our own ability and the "all things are possible" promise of God. God's grace more than compensates for our lack of ability. With or without the thorn.

GOOD SUFFERING

Many years ago, a wise counselor told me, "God doesn't waste good suffering." Strange statement, right? How can suffering be good?

Over the years I have become convinced through countless interactions with suffering people that there is indeed such a thing as good suffering. As someone who hates to waste anything, I find it encouraging and comforting to know that God will use every experience, including our suffering, for his good purposes.

The statement implies that if there is good suffering, there must be less good, or bad suffering, and the Bible supports this idea. Suffering can bring forth good fruit in our lives, but it can also make us unfruitful, helpless, and hopeless. In other words, we become better or bitter depending on why we are suffering and how we deal with it.

Good suffering often comes from obeying the Lord and doing what is right. When we choose the narrow, righteous path instead of the easier, wider path, Jesus guaranteed we would suffer opposition and rejection, and this is painful. The apostles of Christ often reminded disciples that they should expect to suffer for their faith; God is pleased with and rewards this type of suffering (1 Pet. 2:20; 3:14).

Paul told his protégé Timothy, "Everyone who wants to live a godly life in Christ Jesus will suffer persecution" (2 Tim. 3:12, NLT). When we become true believers in the Word of God and carry his Spirit, we will want to pursue godly living. If this invites persecution from unbelievers, we face this suffering with joy because it is temporary, while the "better things waiting" will last forever (Heb. 10:34, NLT).

Paul takes this further, claiming, "We must suffer many hardships to enter the kingdom of God" (Acts 14:22). He said this to *encourage* the believers! It is just as encouraging today to know that when we endure suffering for Christ, we demonstrate our citizenship in his kingdom and our alliance with its distinct values (2 Thess. 1:5). Good suffering follows and imitates Christ as Lord and King and teaches us to serve him faithfully in all seasons.

Good suffering identifies us with Christ's suffering, death, and resurrection. As children of God and joint heirs with Christ, we inherit his glory. But this requires that we be also willing to share in his sufferings. Paul assures us that whatever we may suffer now will seem small and insignificant when we come into the full glory of our union with Christ. (Rom. 8:16–18).

We suffer *with* Christ, "sharing in his death" and, in time, his resurrection life (Phil. 3:10–11). Peter taught Christ-followers to rejoice when we experience "fiery trials" because they make us "partners with Christ in his suffering," noting that we will have the wonderful joy of seeing his glory when it is revealed to all the world (1 Pet. 4:12–13, NLT).

Good suffering connects us to others who are suffering. As one body, the Scriptures admonish all members to rejoice with the rejoicing and suffer with the suffering. Good suffering is shareable. We're not to leave our brothers and sisters alone in their suffering but are to join them in it. This is how we produce "harmony among the members" and care for one another (1 Cor. 12:25–27).

We can do this because we have first been comforted by God. Good suffering elicits the help and comfort of God, who is with us in all our troubles (Ps. 91:15). Because God our Father is so ready to help us, we can help each other endure suffering without being crushed by it (2 Cor. 1:4–6). And because Jesus our High Priest suffered and was tested in all ways that we are tested, "he is able to help us when we are being tested" (Heb. 2:17–18).

Good suffering brings us to the feet of Jesus. There is a marvelous story of a woman who hemorrhaged for twelve years and suffered greatly. We know her story because eventually she squeezed through the crowd as Jesus passed by and touched the hem of his garment. She knew she had been instantly healed. Her desperation had led her to just the right place (Mark 5:25–27).

Similarly, when we suffer pain and hardship in life, we are instructed to pray (James 5:13) and seek him with our whole hearts. In comfortable, safe times, we might neglect our devotion to Jesus, forgetting to bring everything to him. Good suffering humbles us and reveals our need to come boldly and constantly to his throne of grace (Mark 5:25–27).

The admonition embedded in this message about good suffering is that the Christian should only suffer for being and doing good, and not evil. Sin usually brings suffering, and this type of suffering brings no reward with it. But good suffering brings great reward, including the maturing of the fruit of patience (James 1:2–4).

Also, we learn from the Israelites in the wilderness that whining and complaining is *not* how we are to endure suffering. We all have very legitimate causes for suffering in this world, but we are to suffer differently from those who are without hope (1 Thess. 4:13). This is good suffering.

EMOTIONAL BRUISES

Sometimes I notice a bruise on my body and can't remember how, when, or where I received the injury. Was I looking at my phone and walked into a doorjamb? Or did I hit my shin on the dishwasher door when it was open? If I think about it long enough, I might remember.

If the injury isn't serious, it doesn't really matter how it happened. But if I notice several random bruises at the same time, it might signal that it's time for me to slow down and pay attention to how I'm moving through the activities of my life.

This applies to emotional bruises too. This world, especially our relationships with people, can batter us sometimes. When we pay attention to current events, transact business with people, or navigate through cultural land mines, we can feel emotionally sore by the end of the day. Cruelty, tragedy, conflict, and injustice pack a punch, even when they are not happening directly to us.

And it's not just the "outside" world that batters us. In fact, we often get *more* injured by interactions with our brothers and sisters inside our circle than by those outside of it. Sad, but true. On strictly a human level, it is the ones closest who can hurt us the most.

In the garden of Gethsemane, our Messiah was praying and preparing for the agony he was about to endure. He asked a few of his close disciples to pray and watch with him. Was that asking a lot? It doesn't seem so, but they just couldn't stay awake. How disappointing. And on the same night, to know that one of them, Peter, would deny three times even knowing him! The Scripture doesn't say, but

I bet that bruised the Lord's heart more than it did for hundreds of strangers to turn away from following him.

Jesus submitted to lashes, thorns, and scorn and mocking by the Romans and the Sanhedrin. But he also endured the emotional bruises of rejection, denial, and betrayal by his friends and relatives. Who was at the foot of the cross, willing to lock eyes with him in his last moments? A handful of women, a thief, a centurion, one of the Twelve, maybe a few other stragglers at the dreaded scene of his Passion. Jesus didn't have many loyal friends left.

I never have and never will experience anything that excruciating. Mercifully, I am not pierced, tortured, or whipped, physically or emotionally. I only receive relatively minor bruises that fade away with time and don't leave scars. But when I sensed recently that I had been more seriously bruised by someone who loves me, it registered as vital information about both the health of my own soul and the soundness of our relationship.

We teach people how to treat us, so I had to own my part. And I had to reflect upon and take responsibility for the bruises I may have inflicted upon this person as well. We cleared the air and made new agreements about how to better communicate about sensitive topics between us without inflicting injury. This takes courage, but I've found it's well worth it.

If emotional bruising is only occasional, and not a pattern, I will consider it an anomaly. It could be that my associate is having a difficult day or is projecting another's offense onto me momentarily, even unconsciously. I will take the blow. The Lord does this all the time for all of us, and we do well to imitate him.

But when I perceive a pattern has developed, I have learned to slow down and communicate. To value the relationship enough to acknowledge the injury, bind up the wound, and refresh the love and connection between us. To look at the bruises together, however small, and learn from them.

This is what Jesus did with Peter on the beach after Jesus's resurrection. Three times Peter had denied him. Three bruises. Three times Jesus asked, "Peter, do you love me?" In this strange dialog,

Jesus conveyed forgiveness, understanding, and valuing of his friend, despite his betrayals. To restore him, Jesus simply said, "Feed my sheep" (John 21:17).

Jesus challenges us as his friends and followers to learn the lessons of our emotional bruises, to heal and forgive quickly, and to get on with the calling to love people well—when they deserve it and especially when they don't.

GRIEVING WITH THE HEAD AND WITH THE HEART

The story of the raising of Lazarus from the dead in John 11 is one of the most fascinating and exhilarating stories of the Gospels. A beloved friend of Jesus had been dead for four days, his body beginning to decompose, when Jesus called him back to life. His friends removed his grave clothes, and he received another chance at life as a resurrected human being.

This event foreshadows in Scripture the resurrection power that Jesus promises will raise us up at the time the Father has appointed. Lazarus eventually died again but will rise again when Jesus returns. We also will die once, if he tarries, and we who have trusted in Christ will rise with him when the trumpet sounds. These truths from the story are powerfully comforting and meaningful.

But there are other meanings to apply from the story as well. Some of them come to light in the interactions of Jesus with the two sisters of Lazarus, Mary and Martha. They reveal much about the ministry of Jesus in both his divinity and his humanity. They also reveal much about how our minds and hearts respond when we encounter great loss.

Jesus had heard about Lazarus's death two days earlier, and determined to go to Judea, but he waited two more days to depart. When the disciples reminded him of the danger he faced from the Jews in

Judea, Jesus spoke to them about walking in the light. Walking in the light for him meant carrying out his next mission: to raise his friend from the dead. The disciples were confused, but they journeyed on with him.

Jesus first encountered Martha, who rushed out alone to meet him on the road. She cried, "If you had been here, my brother would not have died. But I know that even now God will give you whatever you ask" (John 11:21-22). Jesus replied plainly, "Your brother will rise again" (V.23). This began a brief dialogue about resurrection. Martha in her grief was attempting to comprehend her brother's death using the only theology of death that she knew.

Martha focused on what she had learned and believed: that there is a resurrection day, and her brother would rise on that day. Jesus responded, "I am the resurrection and the life. Whoever believes in me, though he die, yet shall he live," (v.25, ESV). Jesus, in his divinity, amended her theology with the gospel of the kingdom. Jesus came as God made flesh to bring resurrection life, yesterday, today, and forever. He revealed to her mind enough to help her make sense of things at her most painful moment.

This is the same Martha that we know as a worker, a doer, a servant who could become distracted by her serving. She was a good woman who we might surmise functioned primarily from her head. She sought understanding, and in his divinity, Jesus provided it. This is how he loved Martha.

Mary was a different story. Mary remained at the house, surrounded by Jews who had traveled to Bethany to console her. Mary, we know from Luke 10, is the one who chose to sit at Jesus's feet, gazing up adoringly at him, taking in every word. John tells us parenthetically that this was also the same Mary who would "waste" an entire flask of expensive perfume on Jesus's feet and wipe them with her hair.

Mary was a deeply emotional person. She led from her heart, not her head. When Mary heard that Jesus was coming, she ran to him, followed by the other mourners. She fell at his feet and said exactly what Martha had said: "Lord, if you had been here, my brother would not have died" (v.32).

Jesus responded quite differently to Mary. He was "deeply moved in spirit and troubled" (v.34). Without explanation, he told Mary to take him to the gravesite. This is where we encounter the shortest sentence in the Bible: "Jesus wept" (v.35). Jesus did not engage in theological discourse with Mary. He didn't talk about resurrection. In his humanity, he simply joined with her in her grief. He empathized, all the while knowing that soon all those present would be amazed, their sorrow turned to joy, as they saw Lazarus walk out of the tomb. This is how Jesus loved Mary—by weeping with her.

This story supports the view that there is no right or wrong way to grieve. All who have experienced deep grief know that it can be a very messy process. Grief comes in waves or, according to Elisabeth Kübler-Ross, in stages. Sometimes we wrestle with our understanding, debating and bargaining with God in search of answers that we hope will bring comfort. Sometimes we are flooded in our emotions, barely able to put one foot in front of the other. Sometimes we are Martha, sometimes Mary. Jesus, because he is both God and man, knows how to love us perfectly in either case.

Isn't it wonderful that Jesus ministers to us in our grief, in our heads and in our hearts? Being well acquainted with sorrow, he accompanies us through it all, bringing understanding and consolation if we will allow him. How precious is the heart of Jesus, and the way he loves us so personally and perfectly!

SITTING IN THE ASHES

Most people, even those who know little of the Bible, have heard of Job, and connect his name to great loss and suffering. He's the poster child for the apologetic question of why God allows bad things to happen to good people. But that is not my focus here.

My focus is on how Job's three friends attended to him when they heard of his overwhelming losses. Job's friends are famous in the story for being "miserable comforters" (Job 16:2), but they didn't start out that way. These friends get a bad rap by most Bible teachers. I want to give them credit for what they did well and encourage us to follow that example. Then, of course, there needs to be a word of caution about how and when they *stopped* being helpful.

Job lost everything but his wife and his life. He suddenly lost all ten of his children, all of his servants, all of his livestock, all of his assets, and even his health. He began to curse the day he was born.

Job's three friends, Eliphaz, Bildad, and Zophar, heard of the calamity that had befallen him. These men "set out from their homes and met together by agreement to go and sympathize with him and comfort him" (2:11). This is the first thing they did right. They came. They traveled some distance, leaving their own families and businesses to bring love and comfort to their friend. Their intentions appear right and good.

When these friends saw Job from far off, they didn't even recognize him. That's how devastated he was, sitting in the ashes and scraping with a shard of pottery the painful sores covering his entire body

(2:7). Their response was the second right thing they did: "…They began to weep aloud, and they tore their robes and sprinkled dust on their heads" (2:12). Job's friends didn't stand at a distance feeling sorry for him. They joined him in his grief. They took it upon themselves.

The third thing they did is the most beautiful and praiseworthy. "Then they sat on the ground with him seven days and seven nights. No one said a word to him because they saw how great his suffering was" (2:13). They sat in the ashes with him. How many of us have done that? I've never put all else aside, forsaking all other concerns, keeping silent for an entire week to be fully present with a grieving friend. Have you?

Contrast that with Job's wife. Her counsel to her husband was to let go of his integrity and to "curse God and die" (2:9). We must excuse her because she had lost everything too. She clearly was incapable of bringing any comfort. The text doesn't say, but I hope some friends showed up for her as well. As for Job, his friends stepped in and, with their silent presence, they waited and shared the burden of grief.

When did these friends start to go wrong? As soon as they started talking. They started explaining things. They lectured Job in theology. They impugned Job's integrity. They condescended in self-righteous indignation. They rebuked him as he cried out to God, desperately trying to make sense of things for himself. They accused him of presumption and arrogance. Worst of all, they made him feel alone and forsaken. These friends, with their many words, undid the beautiful ministry they had practiced sacrificially for those seven days and nights.

The lesson is obvious. When we have friends who are experiencing great grief and loss, Scripture admonishes us to go to them, to suffer with them, to uphold them, and to help them carry their heavy burdens (Gal. 6:2; Rom. 12:15). We quietly pray and cry out to God with them. We simply stay present.

We wait to speak until we know we have a word from God that will speak truth in the right way and at the right time. We are exceedingly gentle and patient. We put their needs ahead of our own. This may mean that we keep our mouths shut and our opinions to ourselves for a very long time. There is a time for theological arguments, but this is not it.

Grieving friends need our loving presence. They need for us to be willing to sit in the ashes with them, so they know they are not alone.

Job's Tormenters, William Blake, 1793

THE STORIES WE TELL

A dozen years ago, I went through one of those perfect storms of life that had me reeling. Do you know what I'm talking about? You think you're doing a decent job of coping with difficult circumstances, and then life takes a few more blows at you and you start to drown.

I lost my parents within six months of each other, while also dealing with a stressful, dysfunctional work environment. And this was when our family was still adjusting to our new surroundings in Texas after moving from a small town in West Virginia. I had seriously underestimated the potential impact of that much change and loss all at once.

The hardest part was that I felt very alone. We hadn't had time to build a support system yet. To top it all off, my husband had a sudden onset of severe anxiety that required lots of mind-numbing medications. He wasn't fully capable of grieving and growing with me through these very sad and significant events.

Throughout that time, each week a colleague and I commuted together about an hour across town for staff meetings at the main office of our company. On our way home one evening, I poured out my lament to my friend, telling her my complicated tale of woe. When we arrived at the lot where she had left her car, I turned to her and apologized for talking so much. She's a lovely, patient fellow counselor, so of course she told me she had been happy to listen. But I heard myself say to her, "No, I'm boring myself with the story I've been telling. I need to find a new story to tell." This was a turning point.

You see, as a counselor drawn to cognitive therapies, I've been telling clients for years that it isn't the events in our lives that cause most of our emotional distress, but what we believe about them. Suffering comes in the stories we tell ourselves and others. Our stories either keep us in the wreckage of the past or turn us toward a future that is braver and more hopeful.

I'm not saying that we ignore or deny our pain. To the contrary, it is important to acknowledge it, and call it by name. But when we find ourselves repeating and rehearsing the story, and staying depressed and stuck, this might be a clue that it's time for a new story.

Scripture comes to life on this topic of the stories we tell. The Bible is full of stories. Stories of catastrophes and victories, war and peace, bondage and deliverance, sickness and healing, betrayal and reconciliation, sin and forgiveness, judgment and grace. They are stories about broken, flawed people—people like us—in their journeys with God.

Often in the Psalms, the beloved David cries out to God about his story, complaining about his hardships and pain. I love the vulnerability of David's laments, and I love even more how he responds to his own complaints with declarations of the strength and courage he possesses because of his prior history with God. He enters the secret place—his sanctuary with God—and gazes into his face. David acknowledges that he finds himself "in a dry and weary land where there's no water" (Psalm 63:1); but then he begins praising God. The new story he tells is this:

> "I will praise you as long as I live,
>   and in your name I will lift up my hands.
> I will be fully satisfied as with the richest of foods;
>   with singing lips my mouth will praise you." (v. 4-5)

There are dozens of examples like this in the Psalms of telling one story, and then pivoting into a new story about the same reality, one with a new plot and different outcome.

The apostle Paul provides a great New Testament example of

choosing the right story to tell. Paul experienced multiple dire circumstances. He knew very well the cost of taking up his cross to follow the call of Christ. He shared with the churches some of his sufferings for the sake of his ministry to spread the gospel:

> Five times I received from the Jews the forty lashes minus one. Three times I was beaten with rods, once I was pelted with stones, three times I was shipwrecked, I spent a night and a day in the open sea, I have been constantly on the move. I have been in danger from rivers, in danger from bandits, in danger from my fellow Jews, in danger from Gentiles; in danger in the city, in danger in the country, in danger at sea; and in danger from false believers. I have labored and toiled and have often gone without sleep; I have known hunger and thirst and have often gone without food; I have been cold and naked. Besides everything else, I face daily the pressure of my concern for all the churches. (2 Cor. 11:24-28)

Paul faced LOTS of dangers! Add sleeplessness, hunger, thirst, cold, and nakedness. He concludes with his work stress, stewarding the churches he had planted throughout the Roman Empire.

What a story, or bunch of stories Paul could tell! Yet this was the meaning he pulled from all of that suffering: "I delight in weaknesses, in insults, in hardships, in persecutions, in difficulties. For when I am weak, then I am strong" (2 Cor. 12:10). This same man told us that as believers we can do all things through Christ's strength working in us (Phil. 4:13). He proclaimed that whatever his circumstances, he had learned to find contentment in the Lord (Phil. 4:11).

Paul vowed that even when old and tired, he would keep pressing forward until receiving "the prize of the high calling of God in Christ Jesus" (Phil. 3:14, KJV). Check out Philippians chapter 1, where Paul rejoices in his imprisonment, interpreting it not in terms of how it affects him but in terms of how it advances the gospel. He will run his race until he crosses the finish line. Paul was a master of relating the story of his experiences in a way that would glorify Christ and encourage other believers.

David and Paul (and many other Bible heroes) provide examples of acknowledging, explaining, enduring, and coming through victoriously by choosing to tell a story that makes God the hero.

As we go through tumultuous, difficult times, let us not get stuck on a narrative that leaves us frustrated and discouraged. Let us go, like David, into the secret place, abiding there until we can hear God whisper into our spirits a new story. And then let us look for opportunities to share our encouraging, life-giving stories with one another.

10

IN A TIME OF PLAGUE AND UNREST

*Dear friends, don't be surprised at the fiery trials you are
going through, as if something strange were happening
to you…for these trials make you partners with Christ
in his suffering, so that you will have the wonderful joy
of seeing his glory when it is revealed to all the world.*

1 Peter 4:12-13, NLT

The year of our Lord 2020 brought many unwelcome surprises to this world. COVID-19, which had begun to manifest and infect people throughout the year before, evolved into an epidemic and then a pandemic. Families, businesses, schools, health-care facilities, restaurants, travel, churches were all impacted—no segment of our society was untouched by this virus and the fear and dread surrounding it. It changed us as individuals, and it changed our cultures and ways of life.

Concurrently in America, racial tension and violence began to escalate. Though this had been building anyway, new waves of anger were triggered by news of the killing of Black men by White police officers. People began forming bubbles of bias, where they only sought news and information that matched their pre-existing emotions and political positions.

I believe in imparting Scripture in these distressing circumstances. This is a time for well-reasoned, wholehearted apologetics of the Christian faith. Only the gospel of Jesus Christ can adequately answer the human need for understanding and comfort when surrounded by danger and death.

SAFETY IN ROUGH WATERS

We have all been contending in our own ways with the surreal state of affairs brought on by a vicious, invisible virus in 2020. Medical experts used the best of the science available to project likely outcomes in various locations. Meanwhile, government officials at all levels still scramble to do the right thing to protect their people, with little confidence of what that right thing is.

Businesspeople, workers, and investors watched helplessly as their financial security slipped away. Families, colleagues, church members, and friends learned new ways of staying connected while keeping their distance. And of course, career politicians scouted for ways to exploit our collective misfortune for the advancement of their own agendas. Scripture comes to life in these peculiar circumstances, connecting us to the apostle Paul when he experienced his own perilous set of trials.

The last chapters of Acts document Paul's challenging journey to Jerusalem, which he undertook against the wishes of about everyone who knew and loved him. The Holy Spirit warned him repeatedly that he would face prison and many hardships there (Acts 20:23). His response? "I am ready not only to be bound but also to die in Jerusalem for the name of the Lord Jesus" (Acts 21:13). Never has mortal man been more determined to finish his course and ministry, whatever the cost.

Sure enough, he did not experience a warm welcome from the Jews at Jerusalem. They plotted day and night to ambush and kill him. Nevertheless, he resolutely testified about Jesus to Jews in the temple, to the mob outside, and to the Sanhedrin.

For his safety, officials whisked Paul away by night to Caesarea, where he witnessed to two governors. Neither of these governors found probable cause to arrest Paul, but they imprisoned him anyway, to appease the Jews" (Acts 24:27). There are purely political animals in every place and generation, I guess.

Eventually, because the Jews would not cease harassing and threatening him, Paul appealed to Caesar. Once that happened, all the questioning stopped, as it does on cop shows when the suspect asks for a lawyer. Governor Festus declared, "You have appealed to Caesar; to Caesar you will go" (Acts 25:12).

You may already detect some parallels to the political dynamic in America. But here is where the application to our current dilemma gets most interesting. Paul was to be transported to Rome on a cargo ship under armed guard, surrounded by pagan crewmen. Though the centurion in command treated Paul kindly, Paul was not among brothers and sisters in the Lord. Also, winter was coming on, so the weather was unpredictable. No one could ensure safe passage all the way to Rome.

Analysis of the rest of the story could be a basis for a dissertation for a student of sailing. The commander and the sailors ignored Paul's advice to wait in safe harbor and sailed headlong into a ferocious storm. They tried every sailing technique in the book to save the ship from sinking or wrecking. They girded the ship with ropes, pulled anchors, dropped anchors, trimmed sails, loosened sails, jettisoned cargo, threw tackle overboard, and tried to escape on lifeboats. Finally, they just figured they were going to die, and stopped eating.

I am far from knowledgeable about sailing techniques, but I do know something about human behavior, with and without the influence of the Holy Spirit. Isn't it strange that when we are ignorant of or disobedient toward the will of God, we will try every natural means to solve our problems, but they rarely succeed?

Paul was an apostle who had learned to hear from the Spirit very clearly. Luke often mentions the Spirit's intervention in Paul's itinerary by an angel, a dream, or direct revelation. Often his plans changed without notice.

But on this miserable boat ride, what Paul knew without a doubt was that he was going to make it to Rome to appear before Caesar. Therefore, he could say definitively that all who were with him would also survive the trip. They just needed to stay with the ship and listen to the Lord's counsel through him.

Paul's demeanor remained calm, gracious, and confident throughout the trip. He reminds us of Jesus, sleeping on the back of a different ship before being awakened to calm a different storm. This is how Paul brought comfort to the distraught seamen:

> After they had gone a long time without food, Paul stood up before them and said: "Men, you should have taken my advice not to sail from Crete; then you would have spared yourselves this damage and loss. But now I urge you to keep up your courage, because not one of you will be lost; only the ship will be destroyed. Last night an angel of the God to whom I belong and whom I serve stood beside me and said, 'Do not be afraid, Paul. You must stand trial before Caesar; and God has graciously given you the lives of all who sail with you.' So keep up your courage, men, for I have faith in God that it will happen just as he told me. Nevertheless, we must run aground on some island." (27:21–26)

It happened exactly as God told Paul it would. They landed safely on the island of Malta and the residents greeted them warmly. The crewmen watched as Paul was unharmed by a viper's bite and while he healed many sick islanders by the miraculous power of God.

Here is the gist. Can you or I say, "I have faith in God" that whatever he has willed for us will come to pass? If we can hold onto our faith, whatever "nevertheless" might follow, we can keep our peace.

We are likely to face financial loss before the calamities of our day are over. People we know may get sick. Most will recover, but we will hear of those who do not. Will this shake our confidence in the goodness of God? Or will it serve to confirm it?

Paul had pagan unbelievers watching him, and though the text doesn't confirm it, it's highly likely that some of them came to the Lord because of what they saw in him. Paul maintained his faith in God's providence and protection in the face of great fear and uncertainty all around him.

Who is watching me and you, and what will they see in us as we weather this storm and the next one?

Crimea sunset, *photo by Nicholay Vorobyev.*

RISK, SUPERSTITION, AND TRUSTING GOD IN THE TIME OF COVID-19

The earth-shaking shift caused by COVID-19 and its variants has us all questioning anew how we manage risk as individuals, businesses, and social groups. For many of us, risk management is not usually at the forefront of our decisions and thought processes. We generally feel that we are safe enough, and we take a certain amount of risk for granted.

For instance, we all know that driving a car is one of the most dangerous things we can do, statistically speaking. But we put on our seat belts, say a prayer, and dodge the ever-present hazards on the road. We have places to go and things to do, so we push the risk out of our conscious minds.

But the virus, and the decisions made at all levels of society and government in response to it, made personal risk management quite a complex and conscious preoccupation. There are myriad variables to consider during a pandemic, but we lack a proven formula to evaluate them. Many of us do not know on what basis to balance risks to our physical health against risks to our financial, spiritual, psychological, and relational health. And then there is the whole issue of surrendering our rights and freedoms to government control in the name of staying safe.

In this troubling predicament, there is a danger of turning to superstition as a misguided way of dealing with the unknown. There are many ways of falling into this trap. Even putting full trust in the guidance of the "experts" can verge on superstition.

We are told that we should look to science for answers, and that sounds sensible. But as one commentator observed, *science* doesn't speak. *Scientists* speak, and they can only deliver tentative conclusions resulting from their scientific inquiries. Unfortunately, these have been proven far from reliable. There is no science, action, avoidance, or magic charm that can guarantee our safety.

Superstition is understood to be a belief in some cosmic or supernatural correlation used to explain phenomena not explainable by logic or natural laws. For example, people will sometimes say that washing their car caused it to rain the next day. It's pretty hard to make an argument on any logical basis for this. If we want to use logic, we'll say it is purely a coincidence. Superstition is a conditioning process in which people make irrational and inaccurate assumptions about the causes of events as a way of coping with life's difficulties.

Many people view the Christian faith as a superstitious belief system among many others and therefore malign it with skepticism or contempt. But Christian faith is not superstition. Christianity is a very *justified* belief in a benevolent, personal, and sovereign God.

Christianity holds that God is the author of life, and he still interacts with his creation in ways that are partially understandable and partially clothed in mystery. The understandable parts rest upon the historically verifiable realities that Jesus Christ lived, died on a cross on a hill on the outskirts of Jerusalem, and rose from the dead, fulfilling multiple Old Testament prophesies. The mysterious parts relate to how our faith joins us to his plan of salvation, and how his grace confers eternal life and performs miracles.

Believing in these things does not increase suffering; rather, it relieves us from the fear of sin, sickness, and death. It anchors our trust in a holy and good Father. As an old hymn states, "Many things about tomorrow I don't seem to understand...but I know who holds tomorrow and I know who holds my hand."[1] This is faith confirmed by experience.

---

1. Ira Stanphill, *I Know Who Holds Tomorrow*, New Spring Publishing, 1950.

In our present dilemma, as in all others, there is solace in knowing that Scripture comes to life. The psalmist sings, "In peace I will lie down and sleep, for you alone, Lord, make me dwell in safety" (Ps. 4:8). He alone makes us dwell in safety. Our lives are daily at risk, and yet we live.

We should follow the recommendations and requirements of our leaders because that is the right thing to do as citizens. In our own risk management, we should use common sense and take reasonable preventive measures based on the data we know. But we should never make a superstitious belief system out of them. These measures alone will not keep death from the door. God has numbered our days and asks us to trust him through each one, one at a time. This is not superstition. This is the gospel truth.

ETHICAL FITNESS
AND THE OVERFLOW
OF THE HEART

D o you consider yourself a good person? I certainly hope so. But on what basis do any of us make that claim? I have a few answers to consider, some from Scripture, and some from the field of ethics.

During a time of quarantine because of COVID-19, ethics compel us to ask questions such as, "Is it OK to visit Grandma?" or "Should we reopen our business yet?" or "Should we consider homeschooling our kids next year?" You may have never considered these to be problems connected to ethics. I would argue that they are.

What is the thought process involved in making decisions like this that affect our relationships with one another? How do we become wiser and more confident in our ethical decision-making? The answer, like the answer to how we get to Carnegie Hall, is practice, practice, practice.

First, let's define *ethics*. A few shades of meaning from *Webster's* include: "a set of moral principles, a theory or system of moral values, the principles of conduct governing an individual or a group," or "a guiding philosophy."[1] Ethics and morality are often confused, understandably, because "moral" or "morality" often appear as part of the definition of ethics. But moral choices and ethical decisions are different from each other in some important ways.

---

1. "Ethics" Merriam-Webster.com Dictionary, Merriam-Webster, https://www.merriam-webster.com/dictionary/ethic. Accessed 23 Apr. 2022.

With moral choices, we choose between right and wrong based on legal, religious, or social expectations. Families and societies reach a consensus about moral and immoral behavior, and individual consciences develop from there. Moral choices don't usually have gray areas. Robbery, adultery, murder, fraud—these are unambiguously immoral choices. An active conscience leads us toward good moral choices, whereas a weak or inactive conscience allows for immoral choices. Morality is not merely aspirational; We are expected to abide by our agreed-upon rules or accept the potential consequences of our wrongdoing.

In contrast, ethics are aspirational. We internalize standards that we strive to achieve consistently in our conduct toward others. When faced with ethical dilemmas, we must choose between the good and the better, or sometimes between the bad and the less bad. Often there is not a clear path, and we must carefully deliberate before acting.

This has clear application in the counseling world. For example, counselors aspire to scrupulously protect their clients' privacy because it is a crucial aspect of professional ethics. But if a client declares he is going to jump off a bridge as soon as he leaves the counselor's office, the ethic of care overrides the ethic of confidentiality. A wise counselor will call a family member or law enforcement officer to prevent harm to human life. Keeping a promise of privacy is a good thing—it allows for the trust and safety necessary for the therapeutic process. But in the big picture, privacy is not going to matter if the person ends his life.

Outside of the professional realm, ethical choices can be murkier. When we ask if it's okay to visit Grandma in the time of pandemic, we consider the state of Grandma's health and the relative risk of exposing Grandma to illness. But we also must consider how lonely Grandma is, how much she needs our company and touch and support after weeks in isolation. FaceTime and Zoom are great, but they just don't cut it sometimes.

If we haven't flexed our ethical muscles much, these daily questions can be very heavy lifting. Rushworth Kidder, a well-known secular ethicist, took a shot at defining what makes people "good" when he stated,

> Good people are good, we say, because they seem to have some conscious sense of vision, some deep core of ethical values, that gives them the courage to stand up to the tough choices. That doesn't mean they face fewer choices than other people. Quite the opposite: Those who live in close proximity to their basic values are apt to agonize over choices that other people, drifting over the surface of their lives, might never even see as problems.[1]

To paraphrase: becoming more ethical doesn't make life easier, because we become highly sensitized to how our words and actions impact everyone else.

I have borrowed Kidder's term "ethical fitness" and his analogy to physical fitness. If we want to become physically fit, we must put effort into this goal. It won't just happen. We put increased demand on our muscles, bones, and organs, and they grow stronger and healthier over time.

It's the same with ethical fitness. The more we exercise our minds and hearts to discerning what is good, not only for ourselves but for others, the more our hearts become ethically strong and healthy. Kidder explains,

> Ethical fitness is NOT mentally passive, nor is it blind impartiality, doling out right and wrong according to some stone-cold canon of ancient and immutable law. It's a warm and supremely human activity that cares enough for others to want right to prevail.

Ethics is for everyone, not just for leaders and professional people. But it's good to know that ethicists like Kidder who consult with leaders in multiple fields have this understanding that ethical fitness

---

1. Rushworth M. Kidder, *How Good People Make Tough Choices: Resolving the Dilemmas of Ethical Living*. New York: Harper, 2009.

is essentially a matter of the heart. But the best ethics consultant who ever lived, Jesus Christ, is the one who taught us,

> "No good tree bears bad fruit, nor does a bad tree bear good fruit. Each tree is recognized by its own fruit. People do not pick figs from thornbushes, or grapes from briers. A good man brings good things out of the good stored up in his heart, and an evil man brings evil things out of the evil stored up in his heart. For the mouth speaks what the heart is full of." (Luke 6:43–45)

I like this simple pastoral imagery of trees and fruit, bramble bushes and thorns. If we have not been cultivating good fruit by making right choices, then there will be no fruit, only prickly words and actions that hurt people. But if we cultivate hearts of kindness, goodness, peace, and generosity, the fruit in our lives will be evident. We become a blessing and a source of sustenance for others.

Mixing metaphors, Jesus also declares that what we have stored up inside "overflows" into our words and our actions. The book of Hebrews tells us that we can become the "mature, who...have trained themselves to distinguish good from evil" (Heb. 5:14).

As we all work together to do good and help one another during difficult circumstances, remember that we are building our ethical muscles. We are in training, preparing ourselves to go the distance in life with goodness and integrity.

FIRE IN THE BONES

In these perilous times, it is a constant temptation to shoot my mouth off about this issue or that. I know I'm not alone in this; we feel our blood start to boil as we read or watch news stories or follow a thread on social media. There is a rising pressure to speak our minds and set people straight.

I've learned to immediately hit the pause button when I feel that impulse to react with my own opinions about the controversies at hand. I've learned the hard way over the years that emails, texts, and social media platforms are some of the worst places to have a constructive debate or resolve a conflict. Attempting to do so, in my experience, is more likely to make the argument worse. And if I do, who's the judge of whether I am right or wrong in what I say?

When clients ask me if I'd like to read the text threads on their phones so I can understand how bad or wrong the *other* person is, I usually will say, "Actually, no, I would prefer not to."

The other day, as I was reading in Psalms, I came to this:

> I said to myself, "I will watch what I do, and not sin in what I say. I will hold my tongue when the ungodly are around me." But as I stood there in silence—not even speaking of good things—the turmoil within me grew to the bursting point. My thoughts grew hot within me and began to burn, igniting a fire of words. (Psalm 39:1–3, NLT)

Jeremiah the prophet, who was persecuted and ostracized almost every time he opened his mouth, said something similar:

If I say I'll never mention the Lord or speak in his name,
his word burns in my heart like a fire. It's like a fire in
my bones! I am worn out trying to hold it in! I can't do
it! (Jeremiah 20:9, NLT)

It's comforting to know that we who have prophetic gifts today and feel this pressure to speak are in excellent company with the prophets of old. The need to speak, given the possible consequences, can feel like a fire shut up in the bones. There is an urgent need for release.

But…we must ask, What, then, *can* I say without sowing strife, and how should I say it, and when and where, and to whom? I can't answer this question for anyone else. I can only share how Scripture comes to life for me, helping me find some answers. I hope it will help you as well.

Generations come and go, and social issues wax and wane. Only God and his word endure and remain the same forever. Because of this, I have recommitted myself to exercising the fruit of self-control in my use of words. As difficult as it is to tame the tongue—nearly impossible, according to James 3:1–9—we still have a responsibility to do just that, as well as we can. If we speak carelessly, James says,

By our speech we can ruin the world, turn harmony to
chaos, throw mud on a reputation, send the whole world
up in smoke and go up in smoke with it, smoke right
from the pit of hell. (v. 5–6 MSG)

According to Proverbs, it is "scoundrels" who create trouble with their words, lighting a "destructive blaze" (Prov. 16:27, NLT). And it is the "quarrelsome" person who "starts fights as easily as hot embers light charcoal or fire lights wood" (Prov. 26:21, NLT). The cynical Preacher of Ecclesiastes warns us, "God's in charge, not you—the less you speak, the better" (Eccl. 5:2 MSG), and I take this to heart.

You may have experienced this recently if you've dared to speak into the swirl of controversy. You had only goodwill, and you offended someone anyway. It seems lately that if we don't speak, we risk accusations of silent complicity with the perceived enemies of social justice. But if we do, we are bound to offend someone, no matter what we say. How do we wisely manage the risk?

The first principle is that as followers of Jesus, we can say and do the kinds of things he would say and do. Jesus brought glory to the Father, comfort to the brokenhearted, conviction to the sinner, and eternal truth to those struggling with doubt and confusion. If our words are in this territory, we can be assured we are on the right track. Holy Spirit, please help us with our discernment of this!

We can preach the gospel of the kingdom and apply it to the problems in front of us. We can tell people everywhere that God is good, and his mercy endures forever. We can say that God gave his Son as a gift, so that *whosoever* puts trust in him is saved (John 3:16), filled with the Holy Spirit (Gal. 4:6), able to come to a knowledge of the truth (1 Tim. 2:4), and set free by the truth they apply to their lives (John 8:32).

We can also tell people, when they ask, why we have hope when there is so much darkness all around (1 Pet. 3:15). We can express a belief that all will be well in the end, because that's what our trustworthy book says. We can answer questions they may have about how Christianity provides answers to human problems when they may have found unsatisfactory ones or have given up entirely.

If we in the body of Christ won't speak of these things, who will? Paul asks,

> How, then, can they call on the one they have not believed in? And how can they believe in the one of whom they have not heard? And how can they hear without someone preaching to them? And how can anyone preach unless they are sent? As it is written: "How beautiful are the feet of those who bring good news!" (Rom. 10:14–15)

We must tell others of the transformational truth we have found in Jesus Christ and the Word of God.

Within the church, the standard is clear: we are to seek to excel in the edifying of others. Whatever we say or do, prophesy, impart, pray or in whatever context we serve, our primary purpose is to build up the people around us, never to enflame them or sow strife among brothers (1 Cor. 14:5, 12, 26). Never just to prove ourselves right and another wrong. If we suffer, we suffer for saying right things rather than wrong things (1 Pet. 3:14–18).

The apostle Paul explained that his preaching of the Good News was not something he could boast about (1 Cor. 9:16). He was compelled from within. He had the same fire in his bones that Jeremiah had. So did the first apostles in Jerusalem who boldly declared, "We cannot help speaking about what we have seen and heard" (Acts 4:20).

We can focus on issues sometimes, and devote time, money, and energy to them—abortion, racism, human rights, for example. It is fitting for those who represent the Lord to confront unrighteousness, injustice, and cruelty when we see it. But our zeal to advocate for these causes must exist within an unwavering commitment to speak the gospel. Our words must be seasoned always with his grace. This is where people will discover true words of hope, peace, and life.

If we follow this rule and people are offended by us, we stand on the same solid ground where Jesus and the Prophets stood. God blesses and rewards suffering of persecution for Jesus's name (Matt. 5:11). If we can't follow this rule because of a lack of self-control, it seems to me we should follow the Preacher's advice and keep our mouths closed.

MAKING AN ARGUMENT

We often hear people these days yelling at each other, full of emotional fury, but unable to make a clear defense for their strongly held positions. Presenting a thesis and a coherent argument to support it is becoming a lost art. We don't all have to be high-level debaters, rhetoricians, or apologists to acquire skill in presenting a case for what we believe and why we believe it.

It is sometimes difficult to discern when it is time to argue a case and with whom. One of my daily prayers has been, "Lord, show me when to speak, what to say, and more importantly, show me when I am to be silent." If I can't state my case on an issue in a way that is honoring to God and his Word, and with the genuine desire to peacefully edify and inform others, it is best to hold my tongue.

What *not* to argue about…and with whom. Scripture gives us guidance on issues that God's people are *not* to argue about. In Luke 9, the disciples disputed like children in the schoolyard about which of them would be the greatest. Let us not engage in this kind of ridiculous argument with our brothers and sisters!

John the Baptist's disciples argued with some Jews about the need for ceremonial washing (John 3:25–26). The Pharisees were always trying to pick a fight with Jesus about his healing people on the Sabbath. I don't know about you, but I don't have time for disputes about religious practices that are not essential to faith in Christ and his salvation. Several times Paul warns about those who get caught up in genealogies or obsess about angels. These are distractions from sincere faith in Christ.

There are warnings in the Proverbs and in Paul's letters about avoiding arguments with certain types of people: fools and heretics. Proverbs repeatedly points out the futility in trying to convince fools of anything. That is what makes them fools in the first place—they do not receive instruction and despise true wisdom.

Paul says about a person who persists in arguing against the commandments of God, "If anyone is ignorant, let him be ignorant" (1 Cor. 14:38, NKJV). He warns Timothy,

> If anyone teaches otherwise and does not agree to the sound instruction of our Lord Jesus Christ and to godly teaching, they are conceited and understand nothing. They have an unhealthy interest in controversies and quarrels about words that result in envy, strife, malicious talk, evil suspicions and constant friction between people of corrupt mind, who have been robbed of the truth and who think that godliness is a means to financial gain. (1 Tim. 6:3–5)

Demonic arguments and human arguments. The father of lies continually stirs up strife and sets up deceptive arguments against faith-based convictions. These then become culturally normalized, so that if we dare to object to what we perceive to be lies, people who promote them will call us names and try to silence us. This is true right now on issues of sexuality, abortion, environmentalism, and many others. It's called "cancel culture."

When we recognize demonic work like this in our midst, we must counter with the correct weapons—spiritual words, prayers, songs, and declarations—to "demolish arguments and every pretension that sets itself up against the knowledge of God" (2 Cor. 10:5). We demolish arguments, not people; we are not fighting against flesh and blood. This is a spiritual calling, and it requires faith, determination, and a good measure of courage.

We don't give in, as Eve did in the garden when the serpent flatly contradicted God's clear direction. God had said, "Don't eat of this tree or you will surely die." Satan said, "You will not surely die, because…" Satan brought an argument, and Eve had no counterargument to demolish his. I don't think there is a plainer example in all of Scripture. We must be prepared to demolish demonic arguments.

Not all arguments are demonic, and certainly not all who argue against Scripture are evil. They may just be inculcated in a different system of thought but are open to an honest discussion. This involves the art of apologetics. This is where it gets interesting and can even be fun.

The best-known biblical example of this skill is Paul's message to the curious Athenians in Acts 17. Paul acknowledges their religious, cultural, and philosophical worldviews, and makes his own case from that platform. He shows the skeptics a path to faith in Jesus Christ that makes sense to them; he can do this because he has taken the time to understand their cultural context. He doesn't yell at them to win them to Christ. He reasons with them, using their own cultural vocabulary.

There are also some contemporary apologists I admire greatly, among them Tim Keller, Lee Strobel, and Michael Brown. What I appreciate about these men is their ability to stay objectively grounded in truth while showing great grace and respect for their debate opponents.

It is a pleasure to watch Tim Keller or another gifted apologist patiently listen to a debate opponent's or skeptic's challenge to Scripture and then respond with disarming wisdom, grace, and kindness. They've learned to make an argument and defend it, using chapter and verse, but not only chapter and verse. They also use reason, philosophy, literature, logic, experience, history, and best of all, common sense. Their opponents stand speechless. Not disrespected, just corrected.

In this highly charged, conflicted atmosphere, it is tempting to just ride with the downstream flow of the cultural current. But if we do, we forfeit our opportunity to offer an alternative to the increasing barbarity and depravity that grieve our hearts and the heart of

God. Let us look to Jesus, Peter, Paul, and the honorable apologists of our day and follow their examples. When called to take a position on a controversial issue, we will do well to learn how to make an argument based on scriptural truth, and not merely our emotions.

GOD USES EVIL FOR GOOD

I was with two other women in ministry at a Bible study, talking about how COVID-19 has impacted every aspect of our daily lives and ministries. It's changed where we go, who we see, how we earn a living, and how we plan our next steps.

It's been frustrating on the human level for sure. But we know that God is at work, and we have a common desire to see what he is doing through it all.

I believe, based on spiritual discernment and Scripture (John 10:10), that COVID-19's effects are at their root a work of the devil. If his assignment is to "steal, kill, and destroy," then it fits perfectly that this virus comes from him, because that is what it has done. Steal lives and livelihoods. Kill vulnerable bodies and kill hope in the hearts of millions. Destroy businesses, governments, social structures, and community life.

If you think that this is a crazy, superstitious idea, then you don't trust the teaching of Jesus, because it was Jesus who identified this as the enemy's job description. Satan, the great liar, loves to bring hopelessness and to steal worship from our God. The more we focus fearfully on the virus and its effects, the happier he is. All that energy is not going toward the advancing of the kingdom of God.

But there is good news. God doesn't just use the good things in our lives to fulfill his purposes. He uses the evil things too. In our personal lives, if we look back at the times of greatest growth and breakthrough, often we find that it was during times of calamity, pain, and hardship. Conversely, when we recall seasons full of "trials of many kinds" (James 1:2), don't we also see that spiritual fruit matured within us as we persevered?

Think about the devastating hurricanes of the past few decades. Recall how individuals, families, neighborhoods, churches, businesses, organizations, governments, and first responders worked together to rescue, support, and pray for one another. God does not delight in the devastation, but he is well pleased when people show their best selves amid the wreckage Satan brings.

Think about someone you know who has received a terrible diagnosis and had to endure months of frightening, painful treatments. In some cases, they emerged on the other side much stronger, braver, deeper in faith, more thankful, and more wholehearted in every way. God received glory and honor for his transforming healing and grace.

Years ago, I facilitated a support group for women who had survived breast cancer. Every one of them agreed that hearing their doctors utter the word "cancer" was one of the worst moments of their lives. They wouldn't wish it upon their worst enemy. Yet each one said that they wouldn't give back the way their hearts and lives had expanded in love and gratitude through their ordeal.

Scripture comes to life in so many places on this topic, but most vividly in the story of the crucifixion. As a human, Jesus recognized himself in the prophecies of the Old Testament as the "mediator between God and men" (1 Tim. 2:5) who would confront and do away with the sin of humanity on the cross. All four gospels verify that he knew he would give up his life, that he would die by crucifixion, and that he would rise from the dead on the third day.

Jesus knew he would drink the bitter cup to purchase the pardon for our iniquity. He said yes to the Father. But isn't it interesting that God used evil-minded, vicious people to carry out his plan?

God allowed Satan to enter Judas, prompting him to betray Jesus to the authorities. God allowed the Jewish leaders to falsely accuse Jesus and unjustly sentence him to death. God allowed the bloodthirsty Roman soldiers to torture Jesus, drive thorns into his scalp, and nail holes in his hands and feet. God allowed Herod and Pilate to sit idly by while all of this happened. God allowed the crowd to shout, "Crucify him, crucify him!"

God is light, and there is no darkness or shadow in him. To create the conditions in which Jesus could take on all our sin—all of it—he allowed people filled with darkness to play parts in the drama of redemption. In the final analysis, we must never forget that these evildoers didn't kill Jesus; Jesus gave himself freely. He could have come down from the cross, but for love of the world, he finished his part.

What can we learn and apply as we navigate through a time of unprecedented tension, confusion, isolation, and fear? What does God want to do with this demonic bug? He's not afraid of it, that's for sure. And he doesn't want his people to be afraid either.

He could be teaching us to represent him in some new ways. Do we continue to speak boldly of his goodness, declaring our complete confidence in him, however things appear? Is he teaching us to trust him more fully to protect our health or provide for our needs?

Maybe he is testing our faithfulness. If we aren't in church to give our tithes and offerings, do we still give? If we don't have a live band in front of us and lyrics on a screen, do we still worship? If we cannot meet with our brothers and sisters to intercede for each other, do we still pray?

He could be challenging us to take up our cross and follow him (Matt. 10:38). When we see the enemy at work, do we go headlong into the work of the kingdom, taking our stand? Do we oppose him, standing firm with our armor on, brandishing the sword of the Spirit, the Word of God?

I believe he is doing all these things. He is speaking especially to his church in this crucial moment. We must respond to his great faithfulness with our own faithfulness.

IN MY JOURNEY, PART 1: PURSUING GOD

*Surely your goodness and unfailing love will
pursue me all the days of my life, and I will
live in the house of the Lord forever.*

PSALM 23:6

In these last chapters I ask my readers to indulge me in sharing some personal stories about how Scripture has come to my own life at pivotal moments, providing much-needed revelation. I am not a bystander to the struggle to nobly live out the Christian life. I am humbly walking this road of discipleship, desperately in need of God's strength, wisdom, and comfort. In Part 1, I give testimony of some of the landmarks along the way. In Part 2, I share some of the things I have learned about this walk with God from my beloved dogs, Scooter and Maggie. I'm convinced dogs are one of God's greatest gifts to us.

KEEPING MY FIRST LOVE

Some believers have a story of Jesus suddenly crashing into their lives and changing everything in an instant. They have a "new birth" day that they recognize each year, the day when the light dawned, and their entire consciousness suddenly transformed. Others have a story of a more gradual awakening to truth through the hearing of the Word of God—studying it, testing it, and finally believing it with their whole heart. Either way, there is a "BC," a life before Christ, and an "AD," after the death of our old way of being. This is the *anno domini,* the year when the Spirit of the Lord came in and everything changed.

I am in the second category. In 1983, I fell in love first with the Bible, and within a few months I had encountered the Father, and the Son, and the Holy Spirit, and fell in love with God. It truly was a romance. Colors were brighter, food tasted better, friendships were sweeter. Peace, joy, and exhilaration flooded my life and soul. I had an insatiable appetite for the Word of God. Since then, I have endeavored to follow Jesus with all my heart, soul, mind, and strength. Not perfectly, of course, but earnestly and passionately.

I recognize that at some point life happened and domesticated me. Marriage, houses, children, jobs, moves, money pressures, stress, traffic, illnesses, relational conflicts…the good, the bad, the ugly, the wonderful. All of it caused me to lose my former intensity and awareness of God's loving presence within and all around me. The wildness of first love became at times a dull and dutiful devotion. When I realized this had happened it made me very sad, and it filled me with longing for my first intense love for Jesus, the wildest, most wonderful person I ever met.

Brother Lawrence writes so simply and beautifully about the constant awareness of the beauty of God's presence, maintaining the intensity and immediacy of our romance with God. He learned to consistently "practice the presence of God." Brother Lawrence's epiphany did not come through study or fasting or suffering. As his friend chronicled:

> He saw a tree stripped of its leaves, and realized that within a short time, the leaves would be renewed, and after that the flowers and fruit appear. He sensed the grandeur and sovereignty of God over all the world in that epiphany, and that understanding has never been gone from his soul since then.[1]

I love that! But how easy it is in our over-busy, over-noisy lives to lose this understanding.

There are some Bible characters who were "wild at heart" (to borrow John Eldredge's phrase) and then somehow had their senses dulled. David is one, looking over the parapet of his palace at the naked Bathsheba. Could it be that he had allowed his dancing, worshipping passion for God to become dull and stagnant, and thought that a sexual dalliance with her might bring him back to life?

Or Solomon, who experimented with every sensual and material pleasure in search of satisfaction and concluded that it all was vanity, a chasing after the wind. Or Judas, used by Satan to betray the rabbi with whom he had enjoyed such intimate friendship and fellowship, his love for Jesus snuffed out and replaced by greed and bitterness.

We who live in the twenty-first century encounter exactly the same temptations: using sex, pornography, or illicit romances to meet our

---

1. Brother Lawrence and J. D. Nelson, *Practice of the Presence of God with Devotional & Study Guide: Brother Lawrence* (Lexington, KY: Johansson Garcia Publishing, 2016).

need for love, stimulation, and excitement; abusing substances to drive away the pain of our disconnection; chasing after experiences and things, hoping to fill the empty spaces within; betraying and deceiving others in an attempt to gain power or wealth.

These sin-addictions will never satisfy for long. From the beginning of our life with Christ until we are eternally joined to him in our immortal bodies, we can only find true satisfaction in our shared love for one another. This wild, heavenly love is what we seek. Let us never grow old or cold and forget our first love.

HE LIKES ME!

When my kids were little, it wasn't hard to fall desperately in love with them. They were perfectly beautiful and precious to me. I felt so undeserving of these living miracles because of my sexually careless and reckless past. But there they were, pure gifts from heaven, entrusted to my care.

I always told my kids how much I loved them. But I tried to convey to them often that I also liked them a whole lot. I still do.

We are almost compelled by biology to love our children unless our souls have been irreparably damaged or hardened by life. But liking them is a different matter. Liking is taking pleasure in their company. When I have the urge to spend time with people, I seek out those I not only love but who I especially like, my children or others. I'm a quality-time girl.

When I think about the Father's love for me, I understand theologically that his is a covenant kind of love. He loves me because I am his, as I love my children because they are mine. Scripture declares that all who receive him possess the right to be called his children (John 1:12), and he lavishes his love upon us (1 John 3:1). I'm grateful to be the recipient of his overwhelmingly generous, fatherly love.

Although Scripture doesn't say so directly, I also believe that he likes me. I believe this because my Father seeks me out to spend time with me. Sometimes he nudges me awake at night. All the time I will give him, he will take—to visit, to minister, to encourage, to exhort, to rebuke, to speak, to listen as I pour out my prayers. Or to simply be still and join me in silence.

My wonderful Father knows all the shameful sins I committed before I came to know him. But this doesn't seem to be a topic of conversation that interests him, because he never brings them up. Instead, he likes to talk about the beauty of his Son and the friendship we share because of what he did for me. He likes to talk about my wholeheartedness and my passion to walk out my purposes in him: to love him and others with all I am and have.

The Father's way of liking and loving me feels custom made. He knows I am a deep thinker, so he speaks to me in my thoughts. I am a student, so he enlightens me as I study his Word. He has anointed me as a musician, so he reveals mysteries as I give myself to worship. He's made me a teacher and writer, so he pours out inspiration for others when I seek his truth. He knows I love the natural world, so he daily shows me the richness of the sounds, smells, and textures of his creation as I am out walking.

But here is the simplest, most precious part. I remember how I loved to watch my kids while they slept, or while they were coloring or doing some other task, and they didn't know I was watching. My heart would beat faster with affection for them. If they looked up, they would return a shy but knowing smile. They understood that they were both loved and enjoyed by me.

Sometimes when I'm engaged in my busyness and concern, I look up and imagine the Lord watching me with great interest and a tender smile on his face. How sweet it is to know that he loves and takes pleasure in me! He speaks my love language so well, making me feel like I'm his favorite girl.

My Father enjoys my oddness, nerdiness, quirks, and vulnerabilities. Because he has, over time, given me this secure sense of his liking and loving, I feel little impulse these days to compare myself with others. Of course, insecurities can pop up without warning at times, but I know what to do with them now. I tuck myself under his shadow and find comfort and reassurance in his covering love.

A NEED FOR BEAUTY

*Those who live at the ends of the earth stand in
awe of your wonders. From where the sun rises
to where it sets, you inspire shouts of joy.*

Ps. 65:8, NLT

Not long ago I served on a prison ministry team that presented concepts from John and Stasi Eldredge's book, *Captivating*. It was a joy to see the women inmates taking in precious truths about their God-given beauty, their desire to be seen and romanced, the wounds inflicted as they tried to get their needs met, and their craving to fill an irreplaceable role in this world.

Jesus spoke through it all, and the participants seemed to grow in their desire to listen and respond to his voice. For me, too, there were moments of poignancy and revelation. One of the sweetest was when I sensed the Lord redefining romance for me, relating it to my hunger for beauty.

I've never been a girly-girl. I was quite a tomboy as a kid. My piano teacher fired me from my lessons at the age of six because I kept showing up late, straight from playing in the woods, with dirty, bare feet. I was strong, imaginative, and adventurous. As a teen and young adult, I didn't fantasize about a great romance with a white dress, or red roses, or a "castle rising in Spain."

I met and married my husband at twenty-six years old. I was old enough, and somehow just wise enough, to pick someone not based on his ability to romance me but on the secure knowledge that he possessed the character strength that would motivate him to provide, protect, and build a family with me. He was also very funny, which was an essential trait. This is not to say that he lacked a romantic side, because he could be very romantic. It just wasn't the most important thing. It was romance enough for me to have a true companion and friend who loved me unconditionally and made me laugh. Everything else was a bonus.

I am not casting scorn upon women who have a more classically romantic bent. I get it—it's an archetypal, fairy-tale, Disney-princess tale—that I really can't say escaped me entirely. There were times my romantic mother improvised on the piano while my friends and I danced and twirled around in old ball gowns from the church rummage sale.

At this weekend event, I intuited that I truly do have a romantic heart, but I don't experience romance in stereotypically feminine ways. I wrote,

> "I see God's romancing love in my love for trees in winter, birds that chatter in spring, the damp quiet of the woods, the ripples of wind on water, the bow stroking the violin string. Romance is the impulse to step outside and find the moon on a clear evening. It is in the smell of wet leaves in fall or the rumble of a summer storm.

Romance is in the tears that come without warning in movies about lovers, and children, and courage, and loneliness, and sacrifice, and loss, and loyalty. Romance connects me with what is noble and true. Romance is what pulls my heart toward the beauty of God, humanity, and creation."

I'm not going to say that I have no need for the more conventional, intentional romantic gestures my husband might think to bestow. His love for me is beautiful, too, and I dare not take it for granted. But I mustn't minimize how powerfully romantic is the Lord of the Heavens and Earth, who "makes all things beautiful in his time" (Eccl. 3:11). His love is the most captivating.

The God of gods, the mighty Lord himself, has spoken! He shouts out over all the people of the earth in every brilliant sunrise and every beautiful sunset, saying, "Listen to me!" God's glory-light shines out of the Zion-realm with the radiance of perfect beauty. (Ps. 50:1–2 TPT)

Lord, I am undone by your beauty, and the many surprising ways you reveal it to my romantic heart.

Beauty and Wonder, Eastern Sierras, photo by Ruth Stitt, 2019

HOLDING ON
AND LETTING GO

I had a week that was more trying than usual for me, at work and at home. Nothing life-threatening or overwhelming, but more impacting and challenging than usual. And I observed some things about myself and how God deals with me at times like this.

Acquaintances might say that I am a rather calm and studious individual. But those who know me better know that I have a passionate, driven, determined aspect to my personality. I have a fire within me and a free spirit. But I don't typically react to things with emotions at first. I am a thinker.

When things come at me fast and furiously, my instinct is to retreat and process. Like a dog with a bone, I have to chew on things for a while before I even understand how I feel or what actions I am to take in response. You might say I have to brood and wait and feel the ache.

I feel so very human and vulnerable at these times. What I've noticed is that God is gracious toward me and allows me to hold on to my troubles for a bit. He allows me to be angry, frustrated, disappointed, hurt, or anxious. He never forces me to let go before I am ready.

God gave us our minds and our emotions. Each of us has a unique blend of emotional responsiveness and intellectual reasoning. We need both. Sometimes we need to take time to get them to match up and lead us to a good decision about what to do next. We must respond with both what *feels* right and what *is* right.

I'm reminded of the story of Jacob wrestling with God all night. At daybreak, he tells God's angel, "I will not let you go unless you bless me;" Jacob receives his blessing and a change of his name from Jacob to Israel, signifying that "you have struggled with God and with men and have overcome" (Gen. 32:26–28). Jacob had previously been a deceitful, self-absorbed man. He became a humbled worshipper in the midst of that contest.

Like Jacob, if I wrestle with God and man from a rebellious spirit and with an ungodly motive, I will lose in the end. But if I wrestle with God to hear his blessing and his wisdom, there is fruit to gain-- the fruit of love, joy, peace, patience, kindness, goodness, faithfulness, gentleness, and self-control (Gal. 5:22–23). When the fruit comes, I realize that I am so much better off than I would be if the struggle had never come. I am stronger, freer, and more at peace.

Another biblical allusion is Jesus contending with Satan in the wilderness. Jesus won, the devil departed, and "angels came and attended him" (Matt. 4:11). Isn't that a beautiful picture? Like Jesus, we are to stay in the fight until it is time to let go and let God move in to bless, heal, and restore us.

The moment of letting go can be so lovely. After this particular struggle, while I was out walking my little dogs and listening to beautiful worship music, I felt that moment come. I was flooded with gratitude for God's fatherly kindness. He didn't yank the bone out of my mouth but let me hold it as long as I needed to. I felt as though he trusted me—that I would let go when the time was right, and that I would respond rightly to his guidance. This gently enriched my communion with him.

Our loving Father knows us so well and deals with us so personally to reveal his good thoughts and plans, when we are ready. Because he is always holding on to us, we can be secure in the letting go.

HOLDING ME STILL

Transition is a normal, expected part of life. In ministry, it occurs when we depart from one assignment without knowing where we are to serve next. This kind of thing can be tough, especially for those of us who are very purpose driven and need to feel useful and productive. We become restless when required to pause from our labors for long.

I admit that I'm a performer. Raised in a family with a strong work ethic, I can hold myself to a ridiculously stringent standard and must always be conscientiously pursuing goals. I'm an incurable list-maker. Mostly, this peculiarity has served me well.

But I've learned that life and ministry are often bruising. As we're busily pursuing our goals—which often involves intense engagement in the lives of other humans—we are getting nudged, bumped, and pressed in ways we do not acknowledge in the moment. Only later do we realize that our souls are sore and tender, and we need to step away and rest.

I experienced this when I had resigned from a very trying job with a mixture of grief and relief. I sat under a blanket all afternoon, allowing the Lord to pour his healing virtue into my aching heart. He told me to be still and let him put me back together.

Thank God there is anesthesia for major surgery. We need the anesthesia not only to mitigate the pain but to ensure that we stay still so the surgeon can do his work. As I stayed still and submissive to the Lord's kind intervention, It felt as though Holy Spirit infused my body with a profound but very pleasant weightiness. I was a statue, held completely still for ten minutes or so in total rest.

I'm convinced that the Great Physician was reaching in and doing expert repair, restoration, and cleansing. I dared not move until I sensed he was finished. His manifest presence covering my body reminded me that he cares for me intimately and individually. He knows what each of us needs. He knew that I needed this evidence that it was really him loving and healing me.

It is not unusual to endure a period of stress in pursuit of worthy goals. But we must recognize when it is time to allow the Lord to tend to the wounds of the world on our bodies and souls. Our Good Shepherd leads us beside still waters (Ps. 23:2). He tells us, "Be still, and know that I am God" (Ps. 46:10).

BIRTHDAY MESSAGE FROM *THE VELVETEEN RABBIT*

"What is REAL?" asked the Rabbit one day.

Real isn't how you are made," said the Skin Horse. "It's a thing that happens to you. When a child loves you for a long, long time, not just to play with, but REALLY loves you, then you become Real."

"Does it hurt?" asked the Rabbit.

"Sometimes," said the Skin Horse, for he was always truthful. "When you are Real you don't mind being hurt."

"Does it happen all at once, like being wound up," he asked, "or bit by bit?"

"It doesn't happen all at once," said the Skin Horse. "You become. It takes a long time. That's why it doesn't often happen to people who break easily, or have sharp edges, or who have to be carefully kept. Generally, by the time you are Real, most of your hair has been loved off, and your eyes drop out and you get loose in the joints and very shabby. But these things don't matter at all, because once you are Real you can't be ugly, except to people who don't understand."[1]

---

1. Margery Williams, *The Velveteen Rabbit,* New York: Doubleday, 1922.

I recently celebrated a birthday and received from a beloved client a beautifully bound edition of *The Velveteen Rabbit*, the classic of children's literature. Somehow, though surrounded by books throughout my childhood, I had never experienced this particular story.

It is clearly much more than a sweet story for children. When I shared the passage above with some friends of similar age (sixty-something) at my birthday gathering, we all got tears in our eyes and then laughter broke out as we acknowledged how our "hair has been loved off," our eyesight has diminished, our joints are too loose or too tight, and we even feel pretty shabby some days.

What comforting words from this Skin Horse! How we need to be reminded sometimes that it's not the stuff the world sees on the outside that defines our value or beauty. As the apostle Peter instructed the godly women who were followers of Jesus,

> Don't be concerned about the outward beauty of fancy hairstyles, expensive jewelry, or beautiful clothes. You should clothe yourselves instead with the beauty that comes from within, the unfading beauty of a gentle and quiet spirit, which is so precious to God. This is how the holy women of old made themselves beautiful. (1 Peter 3:3–5, NLT)

According to the Skin Horse, and according to the Scriptures, those whose lives are consumed with love and grace toward others—even though it costs a lot and wears us down with time—carry a beauty that can't be denied. This makes growing older an adventure to embrace rather than a tragedy to endure.

It looks like this Horse had read his Bible. His description of those who become REAL is a good match for the Bible's illustrations of those who become holy and whole. They give and receive love easily, and they don't make unreasonable demands of others. They will suffer harm to themselves rather than strike back and demand their rights.

These are sturdy people who don't "break easily." There is strength and resiliency. These people aren't hard and brittle; they remain soft and pliable.

If you read to the end of *The Velveteen Rabbit*, you find that after comforting his small person during an attack of scarlet fever, the rabbit is thrown away because he has become germ infested. But there is a resurrection! He comes back to life! And because he had become REAL through his love, he is transported to a meadow where he can frolic with other real, living, hopping rabbits who are healthy and free.

Cover of *The Velveteen Rabbit* by Margery Williams, illustration by William Nicholson, 1922

What a picture of our promised resurrection day! This life is a testing and training ground for love. Those we love are instruments of God to help us become REAL. The real deal. Maybe worn out at the end, but never ugly, "except to those who don't understand." The final reward is eternal realness and eternal life.

IN MY JOURNEY, PART 2: THE ART OF DOG-WALKING

Scooter (top) and Maggie (bottom), photos by Ruth Stitt

TALE OF TWO DOGGIES, PART 1: LEARNING TO FOLLOW

I have two dogs. Scooter is a wonderful older gentleman, a Welsh terrier with manners from the old country. He doesn't say much but has great expressive ears and eyebrows that tell us what interests him and what disturbs him. He is my faithful companion, irresistibly charming and photogenic.

Then there's Maggie. Maggie is some sort of terrier mix that was rescued off the streets of Houston, scared, bedraggled, and pregnant. We adopted her after she had weaned her puppies. She is truly a lovely dog, sweet and smart, still cute and puppyish.

The only issue I have with Maggie is this: when I am trying to put leashes on both dogs in the morning to take our daily walk, she gets so excited that she makes it practically impossible to get out the door. She jumps on me, barks and cries, turns in circles, gets tangled in the leash, and is frantic to commence the walk. It could be an attachment issue from her troubled past. While this hubbub is going on, Scooter just raises his eyebrows and looks at me as if to say, "Oh brother, not this again."

I'm working on extinguishing Maggie's troublesome behavior in all the typical ways that dog trainers recommend. But as I was walking the dogs one morning, I got a revelation about my dogs, and about myself. I act just like Maggie toward God sometimes. I want him to do something so badly, to make it happen, to "get on with it" (whatever "it" is), that I ironically make it more difficult for him to do it. I make a fuss, or whine, or experience an inner agitation.

The people who love me most must put up with my restlessness and impatience—like Scooter must put up with Maggie because she's his baby sister. Sometimes this behavior is a not-so-subtle form of unbelief—a lack of trust that my heavenly Master has a perfect plan and purpose. I just haven't yet seen it fully.

I have been in relationship with the Lord long enough to know and celebrate that he's in charge and that He takes very good care of my needs. He never disappoints me by telling me we are going somewhere and then refusing to take me with him—dangling a leash in front of me, and then putting it back on the hook. But sometimes he does make me wait. And sometimes I don't handle the waiting very well.

Just as I am training Maggie to be still and wait until I am ready to go, I sense God is daily training me. *Be still, Ruth, and look at me. When I know I have your attention and that you trust me to lead you, we will go.* He does this in his ever-so-kind manner, kinder than I have been with Maggie. This is a guiding psalm:

> Lord, my heart is meek before you. I don't consider
>   myself better than others.
> I'm content to not pursue matters that are over my head—
> such as your complex mysteries and wonders—
> that I'm not yet ready to understand.
> I am humbled and quieted in your presence.
> Like a contented child who rests on its mother's lap,
> I'm your resting child and my soul is content in you.
>   (Ps. 131 TPT)

Other translations reveal that the child is content because he has been weaned. He is not needy or desperate for his mother's attention, just quietly enjoying her presence. He trusts that his needs will be met. He is securely attached in a relationship based in love, not just need.

David concludes the psalm with this exhortation: "O people of

God, your time has come to quietly trust, waiting upon the Lord now and forever" (v.3). We are not to decide when and where he takes us or try to pull him behind us as we walk together. He likes to walk with us! But he insists that we allow him to be the leader, as I must be the leader of my little pack.

Thank you, my sweet dog friends, for teaching me this lesson in trust.

TALE OF TWO DOGGIES, PART 2: LEARNING TO LEAD

Since sharing what I learned from my dogs about trusting God's leadership, there have been some new developments with Scooter and Maggie that have served to amplify those revelations and inspire further insight.

On one of our morning walks, I let both dogs off-leash to wander and exercise in a field near our home. (Scooter wanders and Maggie exercises, as you might guess if you read Part 1). Although we were far from the road, Maggie caught sight of a woman walking by with her small dog. Before I could restrain her, Maggie tore toward them. The woman wisely picked up her dog, but when Maggie got to them, she jumped up on the woman and began attacking the dog, snarling and barking. The woman, of course, was frozen in terror until I got there and got Maggie under control. To our horror, Maggie had latched on to the other dog's backside, but when we inspected, there was no physical damage done, fortunately. Even so, it was very embarrassing and traumatizing and could have been much worse for everyone involved.

My husband Rick and I decided to consult with a professional trainer to help us with an array of doggie behaviors, especially Maggie's reactivity and aggression toward other dogs. As we spelled out the issues with the trainer, she began to formulate a diagnosis of Maggie's behaviors and analyze the family dynamic since Maggie came on the scene. As usual, the trainer had to train the people instead of the dogs.

Two things became clear. The first is that we underestimated the difficulty of both dogs to adjust to Maggie's arrival. Scooter was still mourning the loss of our Wheaton, Annabelle, and was not ready to share his space again. Maggie had been through momentous change, loss, and trauma before her adoption, which caused her to be an insecure attention hog. Their prior experiences made it difficult for them to be at peace with each other or to come into obedience to us, their parents.

More importantly, Rick and I had to recognize our lack of clear and consistent leadership. Both dogs had become confused and anxious by our lack of boundaries. As with human children, our dog children required the right balance of love and discipline. We were okay on the love part, not so much on the discipline part.

As we were finishing our visit and devising a training plan, the trainer began working with Maggie, demonstrating some dos and don'ts. In mere moments with Julie, I could see Maggie relax, pay attention, and follow her leadership. It was a beautiful thing. I was immediately much more hopeful about Maggie's potential. Dogs need to know who is in charge. When there is a lack of leadership, they compete for dominance and act like jealous toddlers. They misbehave and don't get along.

I see a spiritual parallel to what happens in the church when God's people fail to submit to the Holy Spirit's leadership. We come together into packs and become hindered by our reactivity to one another. We each come with our respective historical baggage, often hindered by emotional triggers from the past that haven't healed yet. Still subject to an orphan spirit (like Maggie, perhaps), we covet attention, control, or recognition. Like the Israelites during the time of the judges, each one does what is right in his own eyes. This leads to collective immaturity, unbelief, conflict, and lack of fruitfulness. Paul tells us that where this type of spirit dwells; the carnal mind is directing the show.

God always leads impeccably and mercifully, treating us with the perfect balance of love and discipline. If our hearts are his, we should be very teachable. Outer behavioral change, away from rebellion and anxiety, begins to manifest as we fix our eyes on our loving, righteous leader and follow his lead.

More importantly, inner heart transformation results when we consistently experience God's loving presence and trust him each day to discipline us. We can be at peace with God and others, all walking together in his beautiful kingdom. Like Scooter and Maggie, we just need the right trainer: Jesus the "People Whisperer."

TALE OF TWO DOGGIES, PART 3: WALKING TOGETHER

On another walk with the dogs one morning, I got more revelation about God's dealings with me. These dogs are great teachers: my sweet friend Scooter, the older brother and exquisite Welsh terrier specimen, and Maggie, his little sister and our rescued Yorkie/Schnauzer/Corgi mix (I call her a Schnorgi).

Maggie remains very feisty, playful, stubborn, and demanding of attention. She's the most vocal dog I've ever heard when it comes to expressing her wants and needs. She would love to drag me around the neighborhood if I'd let her. She's my turbo dog.

Meanwhile, Scooter, who is always very chill by comparison, has developed cataracts, and his vision is diminishing noticeably. This means that when we are out walking, he is slower than ever, stopping about every ten feet to listen and get his bearings. He'll hear voices in the distance and put on the brakes until he can make sense of what he is hearing and where it is coming from.

As you can imagine, this makes walking them together a bit frustrating for all three of us. I want to calmly lead and set the pace while listening to my worship playlist and communing with the Lord. Maggie wants to rush ahead on high alert. Scooter wants to plod along with frequent stops. It must be quite a sight at times now that I think about it.

My revelation was that I have been alternately like both dogs. Like Maggie, sometimes in my relationship with the Lord I forget to conform to my leader's pacing and timing, and not push ahead. He's not obligated to tell me the route we'll take through life and ministry. In fact, it's much more enjoyable when I learn to match my stride with his. And it is more helpful and edifying to those around me when I maintain an attitude of unhurried and calm confidence in his leadership.

As for my beloved Scooter, I relate to his aging process. I'm thankful I don't have cataracts, but in the natural, I don't see as well as I once did. I find myself relying more on my spiritual senses than my physical or intellectual strengths. I have been trending toward greater carefulness, introversion, and reflectiveness for some time now. I'm OK with this change. The author of Hebrews describes the spiritually mature as those who are "of full age, even those who by reason of use have their senses exercised to discern both good and evil" (Heb. 5:14, KJV). I'd like to be known as one of those people.

I want to keep the energy and adventurous spirit of my Maggie. I appreciate that she's so good at saying what she needs and not hiding things. She'll never allow me to become lazy and skip our little daily physical and spiritual ritual of walking together. Her sweet, energetic nature keeps me connected with her. I feel that God similarly enjoys my zest for life and my consistent desire to spend time with him.

I also honor Scooter's ability to adapt and adjust to his changing capacities without becoming surly about it. He knows how to rest, how to listen, how to wait, and how to take care of himself. His intuition, patience, and grace keep me connected with him. I feel that God similarly enjoys when I am quiet and slow and attentive to his voice.

These beautiful creatures are some of God's best gifts to me. They continually point my attention back to God's character and his faithful love.

TALE OF TWO DOGGIES, PART 4: AGING GRACEFULLY

I've written about things I've learned from my two dogs, insights that have contributed to my walk with the Lord. Now my husband and I are facing the reality that our beloved Scooter is in his final season of life. He's blind and almost deaf and struggling to navigate through his days. You dog parents can empathize, I'm sure. Meanwhile, the other pup, Maggie, who was an emotional wreck when we first rescued her from the streets, has become a calmer, sweeter, more cooperative family member.

In Part 1 I shared that when we first brought Maggie home, it seemed like Scooter (who was in late, but still robust, middle age at the time) rolled his eyes at Maggie's silly immaturity and reactivity. Now the tables have turned. Maggie seems to understand and tolerate that her big brother needs extra love and care. She doesn't object so much to having to share our attention. She accompanies him as he wanders blindly around the yard.

Watching Maggie and Scooter reminds me of my mother's last year of life, when my kids just knew, without being told, that we would be showing up to visit this dear, demented old woman as often as we could. They understood that this is what we do when family members need us. I've never been prouder of them, and I feel a new pride and appreciation for Maggie too.

This is the final chapter in the series because we will probably be a one-dog family for a while after Scooter passes. All of us will have to mourn the loss of such a wonderful dog friend for a while. And even then, Maggie deserves the chance to experience being an only dog—our greeter-watcher-cuddle-bug-in-chief. In the meantime, this season with Scooter (and other tragic events happening all around us) has caused me to reflect upon the brevity and preciousness of life.

This is not a depressive kind of reflection. There is sadness, of course, but it is balanced by love, tenderness, vulnerability, and especially, thankfulness. I'm learning to be more patient and loving (and less selfish!) about caring for my geriatric dog. I pray that I'll care well for other loved ones who might need me in the future.

I'm moved with tender memories of how much Scooter has added to our family, with his show-dog gait, his glorious eyebrows, his spontaneous posing for photo portraits, his singing when we are singing, his quiet company when we are quiet. I've always felt that dogs are one of God's finest gifts to us, and this one has been an irreplaceable treasure.

But my tender, thankful thoughts travel far beyond. I'm so thankful to God for the life he has given me. I'm thankful to be part of his great big spiritual family. Babies are being born; kids are growing and learning; adults are working hard; old folks are leaving, entering into their reward. All of us are sojourners here, endeavoring to make the most of whatever number of days God has ordained for each of us. We are here to support one another through good times and hard times. Of course, Scripture comes to life in this train of thought.

Ecclesiastes, which expresses a very dim view of the human propensity for "chasing after the wind," also very simply expresses the ultimate priority in being human. Here is a portion of Ecclesiastes 12 from The Passion Translation:

> Honor and enjoy your Creator while you're still young,
> Before the years take their toll and your vigor wanes,
> before your vision dims and the world blurs and the
> winter years keep you close to the fire. In old age, your

body no longer serves you so well.
Muscles slacken, grip weakens, joints stiffen. The shades
are pulled down on the world.
You can't come and go at will. Things grind to a halt.

The hum of the household fades away. You are wakened
now by birdsong. Hikes to the mountains are a thing of
the past. Even a stroll down the road has its terrors.

Your hair turns apple-blossom white, adorning a fragile
and impotent matchstick body.

Yes, you're well on your way to eternal rest, while your
friends make plans for your funeral.

Life, lovely while it lasts, is soon over. Life as we know
it, precious and beautiful, ends.
The body is put back in the same ground it came from.
The spirit returns to God, who first breathed it. (v.1-7)

Jolly fellow, this Teacher. He doesn't pull any punches about the losses that come when our bodies start to wear out. But look at the first sentence, the main point. *Honor and enjoy your Creator while you're still young.*

We dare not wait until we have career and family all figured out, or have achieved whatever else we striving to achieve, or have a certain amount of money in the bank. If we acknowledge, honor, and enjoy our Creator while still young, whatever happens from there is a bonus. I write this from my own experience. When we reach a point of incapacity, we need not feel fear or regret. God has been with us throughout the journey and will carry us through the experience of old age and death as well.

I would add to this biblical truth that we ought to honor and enjoy God's creation also, as God does. We ought to enjoy a great meal with friends, or a walk through the forest, or watching the sunrise from a mountain top or a sunset from the beach. God designed us to respond in excited awe at a baby's first cry or her first steps. We have a unique capacity amongst all of God's creatures to cry at the sound of a violin played beautifully, to be overcome with joy in the presence of the Holy Spirit, to be inspired by witnessing a fellow traveler risk his life to perform a heroic act of love.

When we bear children, we know that they will break our hearts many times and then leave us, but we have children anyway. And we continue to allow ourselves to love our pets, knowing that we will probably outlive them and have to say goodbye.[1] All these experiences, painful and joyous, are what show that God created us in his own image. After all, he is the one who loves completely and sacrificially, knowing that we'll all break his heart at some point. He tells us that we are still worth it. Life is still worth it. Love is still worth it.

---

1. We said goodbye to Scooter in 2020, shortly after the publishing of this final blog in the series. Maggie remains our constant and precious companion.

BIBLIOGRAPHY

Alcoholics Anonymous World Services. *Twelve Steps and Twelve Traditions*. New York: Alcoholics Anonymous World Services, 1989.

Augsburger, David. *Caring Enough to Hear and Be Heard: How to Hear and How to Be Heard in Equal Communication*. Ventura, CA: Regal Books, an imprint of Gospel Light, 1982.

Brown, Brené. *Daring Greatly: How the Courage to Be Vulnerable Transforms the Way We Live, Love, Parent, and Lead*. New York: Avery, an imprint of Penguin Random House, 2015.

Burton, Keith A. "Salt." In *Eerdmans Dictionary of the Bible*, edited by David Noel Freedman. Accordance Bible Software, n.d., 1153.

Chambers, Oswald. *My Utmost for His Highest*. Ulrichsville, OH: Barbour and Company, 1963.

Eldredge, John. *Wild at Heart: Discovering the Secret of a Man's Soul*. Nashville, TN: Thomas Nelson, 2021.

Eldredge, John, and Stasi Eldredge. *Captivating: Discovering the Mystery of a Woman's Soul*. Nashville, TN: Thomas Nelson, 2005.

Hudson, Hugh, dir. *Chariots of Fire*. 1981; Los Angeles: Twentieth Century-Fox Film Corporation.

Johnson, Bill. *When Heaven Invades Earth: A Practical Guide to a Life of Miracles.* Shippensburg, PA: Destiny Image, 2003.

Kidder, Rushworth M. *How Good People Make Tough Choices: Resolving the Dilemmas of Ethical Living.* New York: Harper, 2009.

Lawrence, Brother, and J. D. Nelson. *Practice of the Presence of God with Devotional & Study Guide: Brother Lawrence.* Lexington, KY: Johansson Garcia Publishing, 2016.

Lewis, C. S. *Mere Christianity.* HarperCollins Publishers, 2017.

Lewis, C. S. *The Problem of Pain.* HarperCollins, 2014.

Niequist, Aaron. *The Eternal Current: How a Practice-Based Faith Can Save Us from Drowning.* New York: Waterbrook, 2018.

Ortberg, John. *The Life You've Always Wanted: Spiritual Disciplines for Ordinary People.* Grand Rapids, MI: Zondervan, 2015.

Pariona, Amber. "Religious Demographics of the USA," WorldAtlas, June 26, 2018. https://religious-composition-of-the-united-states.html.

Peck, M. Scott. *The Road Less Traveled and Beyond: Spiritual Growth in an Age of Anxiety.* New York: Simon & Schuster, 1998.

Regan, Brian. "Doctor Visit." YouTube video. Accessed April 8, 2022. https://www.youtube.com/watch?v=B-vKVVcw274.

Silk, Danny. *Culture of Honor,* 25. Shippensburg, PA: Destiny Image, 2009.

The Book of Common Prayer. New York: Seabury Press, 1979.

The Merck Veterinary Manual. Whitehouse Station, NJ: Merck & Co., n.d.

"This is The Story of Why the Dove Is a Symbol of Peace and Love." SpiritualRay.com. https://spiritualray.com/why-is-dove-symbol-of-peace-love.

Tozer, A. W. *Knowledge of the Holy: The Attributes of God. Their Meaning in the Christian Life*. Cambridge, UK: Lutterworth Press, 2018.

Williams, Margery. *The Velveteen Rabbit*. New York: Doubleday, 1922.

ACKNOWLEDGEMENTS

So many wise and kind individuals have instructed me in the study and interpretation of Scripture along the way and are too many to mention here. I am thankful to the Holy Spirit, who leads us to all truth, and who sometimes has led me to fellow pilgrims, scholars, and saints to help me along.

A huge thank you to Les Herron, who sat with me for an exceptionally long coaching session, asking me over and over, *"Ruth, what do you want?"* and wouldn't let me go until I said, "I want to write." He was the one who suggested I start a blog and think about how to funnel my hundreds of wants into just a few that I can do with passion.

Much appreciation to Charla Peterson, a fellow worshipper and creative soul who has listened with openness and interest during my journey through the M.Div. and beyond. She has been ever eager to ponder Scripture with me, and to encourage every creative gift in me.

Thank you to Bethany, my brilliant daughter and fellow grammarian, who has served as my editor, creative advisor, and virtual assistant. We've made much progress together! I pray that Scripture comes to life for you, my daughter, in a thousand wonderful ways!

My editor, Gina Mushynsky, improved my manuscript tremendously, and my book designer Steve Kuhn captured the vision immediately and made it truly beautiful.

Jan de Chambrier has been a faithful friend in all seasons. She is my trustworthy confidant, spiritual mentor, wise fellow author, consultant, and role model of a life fully consecrated to following Jesus.

My husband Rick has quietly and patiently watched me on my laptop for years, wondering at times when I'll come up for air. For 35 years he has said, "Yes, do it! How can I help?" every time the Spirit inspires a new project, and this is no exception.

Thank you also to Frank and Sara Little, Kady Hinojosa, Michelle Rahal, Deb Gruelle, Gabrielle Kingsley, Pastor Chris Holland, Pastor Dave Trotter, Brae and Jill Wyckoff, the hope*writers community, and my Bible study friends for your prayers, support, creative input, inspiration, coaching, and love—over the years and across the miles. You will forever be part of my story.

ABOUT THE AUTHOR

Ruth Stitt lives in the hill country of central Texas with her husband of 35 years and their sweet terrier Maggie. She has retired from her clinical role, and now enjoys writing, playing music with her trio, Cats in Hats, teaching Bible studies, working and playing outdoors, and spending time with friends and family.

WWW.SCRIPTURECOMESTO.LIFE

ruth.e.stitt@scripturecomesto.life

Scripture Comes to Life Publishing
P.O. Box 1444
Blanco, TX 78606